THE
VEGAN
ACTIVIST

GET ACTIVE IN ACTIVISM
FOR THE ANIMALS

BY LEE FOX-SMITH

THE VEGAN ACTIVIST

Get Active In Activism For The Animals

By Lee Fox-Smith

First Published 2018 by Epic Animal Quest

An Epic Animal Quest Publication
www.epicanimalquest.com

ISBN 9781718085596

The Vegan Activist
Get Active In Activism For The Animals

By Lee Fox-Smith
Epic Animal Quest
Copyright © Lee Fox-Smith

Follow Lee Fox-Smith and his written work at www.epicanimalquest.com

This Book is dedicated to my friend, Dr Lucy Haurisa who is changing the world for animals with her activism every single day.

Vegan for life!

Thank you for buying our Epic Animal Quest book and helping the animals!

Enjoy the book!

Lee, Rachael & Family

www.epicanimalquest.com

Find our more about our Book Club and
help the animals today!

www.epicanimalquest.com/club

CONTENTS

INTRODUCTION   i

SECTION 1 - WHAT IS ANIMAL ACTIVISM?   1

Chapter 1 - What Is Activism?   2
Chapter 2 - What Is Veganism?   11
Chapter 3 - What Does It Mean To Be Militant?   16
Chapter 4 - Vegan For The Animals   22
Chapter 5 - The Best Way To Help Animals   30
Chapter 6 - One Person Can Make A Difference   35
Chapter 7 - Insults & Opposition   38
Chapter 8 - Be Inspired   45
Chapter 9 - Activism Versus Charity   49
Chapter 10 - Grassroots Movement   56
Chapter 11 - Compassion For All   61

SECTION 2 - GET ACTIVE   68

Chapter 12 - Talk About Veganism   69
Chapter 13 - Leafleting   78
Chapter 14 - Disrupting   84
Chapter 15 - Volunteering   89
Chapter 16 - Social Media   97
Chapter 17 - Letter Writing & Lobbying   104
Chapter 18 - Get A Job Or Build A Career   109
Chapter 19 - Art   114
Chapter 20 - Learning   119
Chapter 21 - Write A Book   125

Chapter 22 - Social Enterprise   134
Chapter 23 - Public Speaking   144
Chapter 24 - Create A Documentary   149
Chapter 25 - Start A Blog   155
Chapter 26 - Start A Vlog   160
Chapter 27 - Start A Podcast   167
Chapter 28 - Animal Save Movement   172
Chapter 29 - Earthlings Experience   178
Chapter 30 - Chalking   185
Chapter 31 - Undercover Footage   188
Chapter 32 - Buying Animals   193
Chapter 33 - Animal Liberation   201
Chapter 34 - Boycotting   205
Chapter 35 - Stickers   207
Chapter 36 - March   210
Chapter 37 - Hunting Sabotage   213
Chapter 38 - Live By Example   216
Chapter 39 - Everyday Activism   221
Chapter 40 - Build A Beehive   228
Chapter 41- Change The World   231

BOOK CLUB LINK   238
ACKNOWLEDGEMENTS   239
ABOUT EPIC ANIMAL QUEST   240
JOIN OUR BOOK CLUB   245
BEEHIVE FREE CHAPTERS   250

INTRODUCTION

After writing our first Vegan book, The Vegan Argument, we really wanted to create something to help people to take their Veganism one step further, and help them to get involved in animal activism. We wanted to find people like us and work with them to make a difference in the world for the animals. Once we make a choice to Go Vegan, we have to Stay Vegan, and then the best thing we can do for the animals is to Get Active in Animal Activism and encourage more people to do it too. So we wrote this book, The Vegan Activist, to help you get active and show how we can all contribute in our own ways to make the change that so desperately needs to be made.

The word 'activism' can conjure up some false ideas for some people, and when we first started to get involved in the Vegan movement, we thought activism only meant breaking into properties and rescuing animals or attending a protest. We pictured ourselves burning down research facilities and running out of the flame-engulfed buildings with beagles and bunnies under our arms. But there are so many more ways to get active in animal activism and so many different forms of it, that we felt a book would be the perfect way to highlight them and show people how easy it is to get involved. There is a form of activism for everyone, and whether you like to stay at home anonymously or go out into the streets and talk to people face to face, you will find something in this book that you can comfortably do to help the animals and further the movement.

Rather than just talking about activism and it's many forms, we have written this book to include examples of things we have personally done and our initial reaction to them. We have also included practical advice so that you can get started right away. When barriers to entry to any endeavour are removed, it is so easy to get involved with new things and meet new people.

One of the best parts about the activism we have been involved with is the people we have met along the way. They have been funny, inspirational, supportive, intelligent, and generally awesome people, all with the same goal of doing their best to help the animals and make a positive difference in the world. When you first Go Vegan, you will no doubt face a barrage of questions, objections, and criticisms and this can be difficult to deal with. But, when you meet up with a group of amazing vegan activists, all this pales in comparison, and you will feel like you have arrived home amongst people who understand you.

I wanted this book to be a mix of ideas, stories, our own experiences, but also a real guide to getting involved with Vegan activism with information about each form of activism, how to get started, and where to find out more information. The layout of each chapter reflects this, so once you've read about each area of activism and find one that you want to try out, you can see how to do it and give it a go right away! Most groups are on Facebook and are easy to find, but we include links to websites, video tutorials, and books by other creators who are influential and skilled in each area.

We hope you enjoy this book and that you will be inspired to act on what you read. We have to get active in animal activism if we really want to make a difference, so let's do it together, let's change the world!

Thank you so much for everything you are doing to help the animals and thank you for choosing my book to be part of your journey. Please enjoy reading, and I would love it if you joined me on:

Facebook: www.facebook.com/epicanimalquest/
Email: lee@epicanimalquest.com
Website: www.epicanimalquest.com

Thank you

Lee

SECTION 1

WHAT IS ANIMAL ACTIVISM?

CHAPTER 1

WHAT IS ACTIVISM?

"Activism is the rent I pay for living on this planet."

- Alice Walker

What exactly is Animal Activism? Animal activists campaign for Animal Rights. Animal Rights is defined as 'the idea in which some, or all, non-human animals are entitled to the possession of their own lives and that their most basic interests—such as the need to avoid suffering—should be afforded the same consideration as similar interests of human beings.'

There are many ways to promote animal rights, and anyone can get involved, no matter how quiet or outspoken they are. It doesn't take any special skills or qualifications, and all you have to be is passionate with the desire to help the animals and make a difference for them. If you can type, talk, or interact with people in any way, then you can be a vegan activist, and you can make a difference. Your voice and words can be heard by hundreds, even thousands of people, and even if you only get through to one person and they decide to go vegan or at the very least reduce the amount of animal flesh and animal products they eat, then you will have made a considerable difference and helped to save many lives.

Being an animal activist doesn't mean you have to break the law, trespass on private property, or cause damage, though there are times when some people think this is necessary. When animals are liberated from testing facilities or fur farms, the only way to save them is to go in and do it physically! This kind of activity is not something everyone will be comfortable with, and although it is incredible, animal liberation is not an essential part of being an animal activist. You can be a very effective activist without ever touching an animal.

Perhaps this is why people conjure up a false image when they think of an animal activist and why some people (including governments across the world) view certain types of animal activism as terrorism. How sad when a society deems the torture of animals for makeup perfectly acceptable but the desire to free them and end their unnecessary torture is extreme.

So Animal Activism is simply any activity that you can carry out that promotes Animal Rights and furthers the cause. There are no prizes for how much you do or how much time you spend doing it. The more you can do the better and the more of us that do something, the more significant impact we can have to help the animals. If every Vegan did one small activity each week, then things would change very quickly. At the moment, we see small groups of Animal Activists working hard to promote Animal Rights while other vegans in their areas only talk about what food they eat. This is not limited to Veganism, as most people like to talk about themselves and would prefer to carry out activities that entertain or benefit them directly. Don't get me wrong, using food as a form of activism is a good idea, but that's different from just posting pictures of what we have for dinner each night.

An example of this is back in Cornwall where we lived for 10 years before beginning our Epic Animal Quest. I joined a small group of Animal Activists that took part in demonstrations, outreach, and protests. Often, there would be 10-15 of us, and it was always the same faces at each event. In the county, vegan groups were boasting 1000's of vegan members, but whenever an Animal Activism event was advertised, the support would always be the same 10-15 people attending. In contrast, anytime a Vegan festival or cake tasting or food-based event was put on, hundreds of Cornish Vegans would turn out.

Now, I understand that people have jobs, people are busy with family commitments and the like, and as I said earlier, there are no prizes here, but, and it's a big but, how much effort would it take to attend just one peaceful protest every one, two, or three months? Pop along after work for one hour? We all have lives, and it is important that those lives don't suffer, but we must remember the animals are losing theirs at a rate of 3,000 every second. If we band together and all make an effort, we can really do something to change this in a huge and unimaginable way.

It is estimated that there are 600,000 vegans in the UK and this is multiplying rapidly. If we base the Animal Activists on the Cornish example (and we have discussed the same figures with other groups across the UK), then we can roughly assume that 1% of Vegans regularly take part in activism. That's only 6,000 vegans actively promoting animal rights in the UK. Imagine if we could increase this to ten, twenty, or thirty percent? If we can turn up at protests with hundreds of people every time we would get noticed, and we would influence others to join, and in turn, we would instigate real change. So I always arrive at the same question when I think about this; why don't more Vegans get involved in Animal Activism and how can we help? That's why we wrote this book, to get more Vegans involved and to grow the number of active activists.

Once people realise that activism is peaceful and non-destructive, I think they will be more inclined to learn more about it and give it a try. Most of the activism is going to involve talking to people face to face or on social media, and lots of people love to talk and share ideas. When talking about Veganism, you will meet people who will question, argue, and object to your lifestyle and ideas. Some people will get angry, and others will mock you. I firmly believe that we have to answer the questions in the best way we can and that doing so is one of the best ways we can help the animals. If we can answer all the questions we are given and put to rest all the objections, then people will be left in a position where they will have to make a decision. Will they carry on with their cruel and destructive lifestyle, or will they make a change? Once people know the truth, they either have to act or live with themselves and their apathy.

One thing we quickly learned was to avoid engaging with trolls. There is no point getting into an argument on Twitter or Facebook or even face to face. It leads nowhere, and we have found we only come away annoyed and wound up. People have to be ready to make a change, and they have to be open to new information and ideas. Whenever someone posts a picture of a steak or a bacon sandwich on a Vegan social media feed, you know they are not there to learn something new or engage in a rational conversation or even a debate. They are there for their own entertainment; nothing else. So we choose to avoid these trolls and don't engage. It's easy to delete a comment, block or ban them.

Not everyone will agree with this, and many feel they need to show the troll for the moron they are and engage in lengthy conversations online. I don't think this is wrong, but it's not the approach we have chosen. We have made the decision to not engage with faceless cowards who's only intention is to upset complete strangers for no end other than personal satisfaction and gratification. We leave them to their hate and move on to help the animals by engaging with people who are capable of talking seriously about Veganism. We don't have to convert people overnight (although that would be awesome), our job is to answer questions and sow seeds in their minds that will make them look further and hopefully make their own connection, just like we did.

Once we decide not to engage with trolls, we can remove many of the negative aspects of animal activism and make it an enjoyable experience. It sounds strange to say this, but when you meet other Vegans, and you work together as a collaborative group, supporting each other, backing each other up, and helping each other, the experience is a positive one. Vegan outreach is an example of an activity that is fun to do. Showing people how delicious plant-based food is and talking about how they can change their lifestyle and make better choices for the animals is empowering, and when people you know go Vegan partly because of something you have done or said, then that is the best feeling ever!

If the best way to help animals is simply to stop eating them, how can we encourage more people to do just that? Well, that's why I think we have to answer questions correctly, rationally, and logically. It's about helping people to understand why vegans choose the vegan lifestyle and why it is better for the animals, the planet, and our health. It's about showing how eating, wearing, exploiting, and abusing animals is morally unjustifiable. The more ways we can do this, and the more people who do it, the greater effect we will have for god in the world.

Anytime you get in a conversation about your vegan lifestyle choice, questions will no doubt be raised. You will often be mocked, laughed at, misunderstood, and ignored, but it's important to be ready for this. You can help the animals by being prepared and having all the answers to any questions people throw at you. Answering questions about things like protein, vitamin B12, and canine teeth, will give you an opportunity to sow a seed in the minds of the questioner. Hopefully, that seed will sprout, and as you water it with more answers and information, it will flower into a compassionate vegan mind. Being a good activist is all about being well informed, and preparation can help you so much so that when you are asked questions, you can give awesome answers.

Many vegans were meat eaters for years before they went vegan. Although I am ashamed to say it, I ate meat for over thirty years before making the connection and committing to helping the animals and going vegan. This is important to remember so that we don't treat meat eaters like the enemy. They are just like we were. I wish I had met a vegan who was able to give me all the answers years ago, and if I was given the information as a child, I think I would have made the connection long ago. The internet has given this opportunity to the vegan movement now, as information is easy to access and easy to spread around. The lies that have been told by the meat, egg, and dairy industries for so long, can quickly and easily be checked and revealed to be false. We can look beyond the facade of the happy chicken on the billboard or the side of the delivery van, and clearly see the shameful, disgusting, and unacceptable cruelty and pain inflicted on animals every day.

Remembering how we used to live, think, and eat is important and I approach people and situations in ways that I think I would have responded to before I was Vegan. Being called names and being told what to do don't work in changing peoples minds, and the approach can actually have the adverse response. But if we talk to people and introduce new ideas and ways of thinking and behaving and out across a reasoned defence, we can engage in better conversations and have better opportunities to convert them to a compassionate lifestyle.

Individuals can make an immediate difference just by making the connection and deciding not to eat animals or use animals for entertainment, experimentation, clothing, or profit. As more and more individuals come together, we find ourselves in a position where we truly can change the world for the better. As activists, we have an opportunity to help people make this connection and the more people who we can help, the more animals will be spared suffering, abuse, and horrific deaths. So let's all get more active in animal activism and work together to make the world a better place for everyone!

CHAPTER 2

WHAT IS VEGANISM?

"We are quite literally, gambling with the future of our planet - for the sake of hamburgers."

- Peter Singer

What Is Veganism? Defining Veganism Correctly - With Video

This post is all about defining Veganism correctly.

Whenever I get into a conversation with someone about Veganism, I feel it is really important that they understand exactly what Veganism is. Veganism is defined by the Vegan Society as:

"A philosophy and way of living which seeks to exclude—as far as is possible and practicable—all forms of exploitation of, and cruelty to, animals for food, clothing or any other purpose; and by extension, promotes the development and use of animal-free alternatives for the benefit of humans, animals and the environment. In dietary terms, it denotes the practice of dispensing with all products derived wholly or partly from animals."

I think it is really important to emphasise that Veganism isn't a diet, it is a way of life. It isn't something to dip in and out of, and I believe that once you commit to Veganism, it should become a commitment for life. After all, when you know the true horrors and abuse the animals face by their billions, how can you ever go back knowingly contributing to it?

Find out more about Veganism by visiting the Vegan Society website here https://www.vegansociety.com/go-vegan/definition-veganism

Practicable

The definition uses the word practicable, and I think this often gets confused with the word practical. Practicable refers to 'something that is able to be done or put into practice successfully.' For example, in the world we live in, can we successfully survive and thrive on a plant-based diet? Of course, we can! And this is something we can all easily put into practice. So if it is possible and practicable for us to lead a Vegan Lifestyle, what is stopping everyone doing it?

Of course, not everyone on the planet can survive and thrive on a plant-based diet. Inuits and remote village tribes being possible two examples. However, there are only estimated to be 370 million indigenous peoples in the world and so that leaves the other 6.7 Billion of us with no excuse! The number of indigenous people is declining as we take over their land for oil, water, and animal agriculture. So the people who some meat eaters use an excuse to eat meat, will soon no longer be living in a way that forces them too and they will be able the make the same choice to Go Vegan that we can.

Promote Animal-Free Alternatives

Once we have excluded all forms of exploitation and cruelty in our own lives, how do we go about promoting animal-free alternatives? How do we work to benefit the animals, our health, and the planet? We can become activists and link with other animal rights activists wherever we are and go out to animal save meetings and outreach campaigns. If none of these activities are commonplace in your area, you could start your own. When we first got to Cambodia, we got involved with others and started what we could where we found ourselves. You can volunteer to work hands-on with animals alongside local charities and promote compassion for all animals in your local schools. Write books or a daily blog. You could draw thought-provoking cartoons, create memes, and join in conversations online helping people who need help with their new lifestyle. These are all small things that we can all do alongside our normal working lives, well, with the exception of the books, these take a lot of energy and effort! This book will go into detail and give you lots of options to promote Vegan alternatives.

Promoting alternatives is as big a deal as campaigning against the treatment of animals by all the different industries. But the two should come hand in hand. While we say one thing is bad, we can put forward a kinder, more compassionate solution or alternative. We often write that we are living the dream in a world full of nightmares, and this is so true where Veganism is concerned. We see disgusting treatment of animals, but then we see amazing people campaigning for them. Businesses are popping up more and more with the goal of supplying Vegan products, and more and more people are seeing the benefits. This is giving us an abundance of Vegan products to champion and promote, and we all need to show our support and get busy helping with their success.

Veganism isn't a lack of anything, and there are alternatives for all the things we need and enjoy. I never think about

Veganism as something that makes me lose out or that it takes something away from me. After all, by avoiding animals and their products in my diet and lifestyle, all I am doing is no longer taking that which does not belong to me. And that is what Veganism is all about, not taking what doesn't belong to us and doing as little harm as possible as we go about our lives.

So Veganism is all about doing as little harm as is practicable and possible and promoting Vegan alternatives. We must show the truth, share the mistreatment and abuse, but also champion the benefits to the animals, our health, and the planet we all live on and share.

CHAPTER 3

MILITANT VEGAN

"I am not only a pacifist but a militant pacifist. I am willing to fight for peace. Nothing will end war unless the people themselves refuse to go to war."

- Albert Einstein

You may have been called a 'Militant Vegan' or a 'Hardcore Vegan' before, but what exactly does it mean to be militant in your approach to Veganism? This chapter will define militant Vegan, hardcore Vegan, and argue why it's not a bad thing to be accused of either term.

Define Militant Vegan and Veganism

Veganism

People often confuse Veganism with a Plant Based Diet, and it's just not the same thing. Diet is only a part of what being vegan is all about. Veganism is defined by the Vegan Society (who coined the phrase Veganism) as:

A philosophy and way of living which seeks to exclude—as far as is possible and practicable—all forms of exploitation of, and cruelty to, animals for food, clothing or any other purpose; and by extension, promotes the development and use of animal-free alternatives for the benefit of humans, animals and the environment. In dietary terms, it denotes the practice of dispensing with all products derived wholly or partly from animals."

As we detailed in the previous chapter, a Vegan is someone who chooses to live their life in line with this philosophy.

Militant

A person who is 'combative and aggressive in support of a political or social cause, and typically favouring extreme, violent, or confrontational methods.'

Hardcore

A person who is 'the most active, committed, or doctrinaire (a person who seeks to impose a doctrine without regard to practical considerations) members of a group or movement.'

Passionate, active, committed, and truthful, these are all words that correctly describe a Vegan animal activist, and attaching hardcore should never be seen as a negative thing. But our actions are not militant. I know people who have been called Militant Vegans. They are not aggressive, extreme, or violent, and the only confrontation they cause is with the truth. I believe that meat eaters will accuse someone of being Militant just because they show the truth and talk about it passionately. No one wants to be told what they are doing is bad, wrong, or immoral. In fact, we don't even have to tell people, we can just show them the reality, the truth, and they will freak out and get defensive. As Nietzsche said, "sometimes people don't want to hear the truth because they don't want their illusions destroyed." We are in the business of confronting these illusions, and that can sadly be viewed as militant.

I would take it as a complement if someone told me I was militant or hardcore. At least it means they are hearing what I have to say! If we really want to change the world and make a difference for the animals, then we just have to speak up, speak out, and be outspoken, and be proud to do it too. The animals do not have a voice that meat eaters want to listen to, so we have to be a voice that they cannot avoid.

Using terms like Militant and Hardcore is just an effort to stop people from speaking the truth and showing the reality of the world we live in and contribute to. If we come across in this way, while remaining peaceful and honest in what we say, then it is not our fault if people find that uncomfortable.

Some people just don't want to change and even know the true horror the animals face and still carry on eating and exploiting them. But other people are ready to change. I know this because two years ago, I was one of them. Now, I meet and talk to people all the time who have shared the same experience as me. If we can keep moving forward talking to and getting the message to as many people as possible, then we reach those who will respond well and who will change for the sake of the animals. These people who will change could go on to be activists themselves, so we have a huge responsibility to find them and talk to them in the right way.

Being peaceful is important, it goes without saying, but can we create a big enough change in the world without resorting to violence? I think this is where Veganism is unique. Vegans are made up of people from different countries, cultures, races, colours, and creeds. We are not a single group that is located in one particular place, but instead, we are spread out across the globe with a common voice. In the past, many civil rights movements have had to take up arms to bring about change, but I would hope Veganism can spread through compassion and rational, logical behaviour. Encouraging people to stop hurting animals by hurting other people just doesn't make any sense to me.

We live in an age where technology such as the internet and social media allows us to share ideas and have conversations. We can show the truth and counter the lies that we have all been drip fed for decades. We can show people the benefits of going Vegan for the Animals, their own Health, and our Planet. A change will be slow, but we are seeing it happening all around us, and it's growing every day. More people are going vegan than ever before, and vegan alternatives are more accessible for clothes, food, cleaning, and hygiene products. We can use the power of supply and demand to affect change in our own communities and everywhere else. We can use the system against itself.

In order to do this, we must first change our own behaviour and use the knowledge to live a more compassionate life and then share it with other people. We have to show people the truth and explain the benefits of Veganism for the Animals, Our Health, and Our Planet. Once we have shown people the truth and explained the benefits, they will know better, then we just have to encourage them to do better too.

I am not a pacifist by any means, and if someone (be that a human or other animal) physically threatened my family or me then, of course, I would attack and fight back. But I do not advocate violent means to achieve a goal that can be accomplished in other peaceful ways. Being a Vegan and choosing a compassionate lifestyle, doesn't mean we have to be pushovers and allow other people to express themselves violently towards us. But it does mean we should practice compassion as much as is possible.

CHAPTER 4

VEGAN FOR THE ANIMALS

"The love for all living creatures is the most noble attribute
of man."

- Charles Darwin

I always say that we chose to go Vegan for the animals and
that Veganism is a lifestyle that will help provide a better future for our children, the animals, our health, and the planet.
It is obvious how Veganism will benefit the animals, but how,
exactly, will Veganism benefit the planet as a whole? What
does being a Vegan mean for the Earth that we all have to
share? This chapter is all about why we have to go Vegan for
the Planet and our environment as well as the animals and
stresses the importance of Veganism for any kind of a hope-
ful future.

Climate change can't be denied, but it is sad to see that it is by many of the people who are in positions of power to do something about it. Money, greed, and power are three of the worst traits of humans, and they could very well be the things that end our time here on Earth. Climate Change Science is a massive subject that is well beyond me and this book, but it is important to be aware of the role animal agriculture plays in it so I want to touch on it here. We may not be able to change the minds of the corporate powerhouses or change how we use natural resources on a global scale, but we can all make an immediate choice to stop eating animals and stop contributing to the damages caused by animal agriculture.

Scientists all around the world agree that Climate Change is happening and that there are a number of main factors that are responsible for it. It seems it is difficult - perhaps even impossible - to predict precisely how much each factor contributes to Climate Change, but it can't be denied that they have an effect. Natural occurrences have an effect on the climate too, and some cycles cause changes over the millennia, but the gross effect of the actions of humans is interfering with these natural processes and causing our environment to fall way out of balance. These factors are:

Human Factors:

Destruction of natural habitats for urbanisation, palm oil, and animal agriculture
Deforestation for building resources, paper, furniture, and animal agriculture
Production of chemicals for cleaning, food production, and ingredients
Production of plastic

Production and disposal of single-use items for packaging
Pollution caused by factory farming and animal agriculture
Pesticides, Herbicides, and Fungicides
Unsustainable farming methods
Vehicles
Use of fossil fuels for Power Plants
The growth of cities and the increase of transportation
Breeding and killing almost 60 Billion land animals each year
for the food we don't need to survive and thrive
Fishing the oceans and waterways removing literally trillions
of fish and crustaceans every year

Natural factors:

Continental Drift
Seasons
The Sun and its behaviour
Ocean Currents
Volcanoes
The Earths orbit (see precession and the 26,000-year cycle)

So what effect will the reduction of these Human Factors
have on Climate Change? I am not sure there is an answer, it
may even be too late, but if we don't reduce our harmful
activity, then we will only make things worse; perhaps even
catastrophic. Robert Swan OBE said, "The greatest threat to
our planet is the belief that someone else will save it." If we
bury our heads in the sand then what does that mean for our
children's future? If we all just take one tiny step and stop
being part of the animal agriculture nightmare, then imagine
how far we will move forward as a human race? Those tiny
steps will add up to miles of progress and lay the road for our
children to march on long after we have moved on.

Ok, So What Is The Answer? In short, I don't have one. I don't know what the solution is, but I do know we can all take one immediate step that will positively affect 7 of the 13 human factors in Climate Change. You already know what it is, we can all choose to Go Vegan!

We can all immediately stop contributing to the problems caused by animal agriculture. Yes, we will still have to farm vegetables and fruit, but the impact will be far, far less. We have written a lot about Rainforests and Soy Production on our website and shown how much food is grown just to feed the animals we eat and how that food (far less in fact) could be used to feed everyone on the planet. With a few changes, we could sustainably grow enough food to comfortably feed everyone on the planet. There are many arguments about Veganism and Farming, and I address most of them in my book, The Vegan Argument: why there really is an answer to everything.

Our next obvious step has to be to stop being so wasteful. Stop using plastic and single-use packaging. This is something I am terribly guilty of and am working on changing. We have reusable bags for shopping, we are about to buy some material bags so when we buy rice and pulses from the markets, we can ask them to put it in them instead of one use plastic bags. We have drinking flasks that will last us a lifetime, so we no longer have to buy drinks and juices in plastic containers. We are sourcing suppliers that recycle more and waste less and choosing to spend our money there while boycotting other more wasteful alternatives. My family and I are far behind many who have been doing this for years. People all around the world are already doing things like this and much more. India has stopped using plastic bags in its capital and is banning plastic across the country, which is amazing!

If other countries follow suit, then imagine the difference that will make?

Berlin has recently opened its first package-free supermarket, and the idea is spreading. I can imagine a kind of package free starter pack, where people can buy everything they need to live a package free lifestyle, buy it once and use it for years. When it breaks or is no longer functional, then it can easily be recycled.

We are looking at ways we can stop being wasteful in general, and I will admit it is not easy. All our lives, we have been part of a self-destructive system and trying to get out of it is, to say the least. Difficult, but certainly not impossible. For me, this is what the Vegan lifestyle is all about. Being Vegan is not just about eating a Vegan plant-based diet, that is only a part of it. Making a choice to Go Vegan started us thinking about everything we do that impacts the animals, our health, and the planet.

We no longer own a car and either walk or use public transport. When we lived in the UK, we had our own car, two cars for a long time, and I would drive to work on my own in one of them. In Phnom Penh where we spent eighteen months, we often saw 4 people all riding on the same motorbike which, in most cases, was a 125cc engine! The traffic drives really slow there too, so the Cambodians used their transport and fuel very efficiently. Public transportation in Phnom Penh is primarily by Tuk Tuk, with the 4 of us riding in the back being towed by a 125cc bike and it's rider. If we were on our own, we would walk or get a single passenger Moto, though I wouldn't recommend riding on these without a helmet. In contrast, as the city was developing and more affluent behaviours crept in, we would see lots of large gas guzzling 4 x 4 Range Rovers often with only the driver in-side, and it just felt so wrong.

In the UK, it is mostly cars just like the Range Rovers, and they drive fast, accelerating then braking last minute; very inefficient and wasteful. But the western lifestyle is desirable, and I fear countries trying to copy it will move away from their own more efficient methods of transport. But, we can choose to use public transport anywhere in the world. Before we left for our epic animal quest, we sold our car and happily went without it for almost a year. It was difficult at first, the children moaned, Rachael moaned, and I pretended it didn't bother me at all; though it obviously did at first. I may love to change and embrace it, but sometimes it is not always com-pletely positive. Once we got used to it though, it was so much better. We walked more, our pace of life slowed a little, and we sought out activities and places we wouldn't have experienced with a car. Our routines changed, I read more during the commute to work, could carry out tasks that gave me more time when I got home, we all chilled out, and we talked more and argued less whenever we went out for the day. No more fighting over who would sit in the front seat or be in charge of the radio. Personally, getting rid of the car was the best decision we made after choosing to Go Vegan.

When we sold almost all our possessions to leave for Cam-bodia, it was sickening to see just how much we had accrued over the years and how much we didn't use. We took a Luton van full of junk to the tip and two loads to charity shops and had a house sale to get rid of whatever we could. Although it was gross to see what we had wasted, it felt awesome and liberating to get rid of it all. We have still kept a lot of the children's toys in storage in the UK, but most of what we had has gone. Now we only have what we can carry in 4 suitcases, and 4 carry-ons. Total weight is 140kg. Anything that we can't fit or carry, we don't own.

It is weird to realise that we don't need most of the things we think we do and this experience has taught me a lot. I still think we have too much and have formed attachments to objects rather than people, but that's what this new life is all about, collecting experiences and friendships rather than items and possessions.

I know this all sounds really preachy, but Climate Change and environmental and global destruction are really happening. If we don't do something, or at the very least try, then what does that say about us? What will we say to our Grandchildren when they ask us why we didn't try to do anything when we had the chance?

All my life I have been contributing to the destruction of the planet in huge ways and still am to a lesser degree. Knowing that for most of my life I was making the planet worse than when I arrived in it makes me feel terribly guilty. I have talked before about the Robert Mann quote, "be ashamed to die until you have made some victory for mankind," and I totally stand by it. My mission is to leave this planet better than I found it and give my children a better future. I don't want to get to my deathbed and look back thinking that I didn't act when I could have.

I have learnt in business that you have to face everything head on. If something goes wrong and you ignore it, then it only gets worse and comes back to bite you at a later date. Things can snowball and run out of control until they form an avalanche that destroys everything in its path. We have to face the situation we are all in together on this planet before it gets completely out of control and we all pay the biggest of prices for our apathy.

If we don't change on a global scale, then things will certainly not improve and can only get worse; much worse. The Oceans could be empty of fish by 2048 (read post here), there will be more plastic in the oceans than fish, rainforests - the lungs of our planet - will be destroyed irreversibly, more people will starve, war will continue for land, oil, and water, fossil fuels will run out, many more animals (including people) will be exploited or killed unnecessarily.

This all sounds very dramatic, like something from a movie, but it is all very real, and it is happening all around us. An hour spent online reading the articles and journals will show just how real it is. Take a walk along your local beach to see the plastic washed ashore, and you will see the sad reality. So our activism is necessary for more than the animals, it has to be. If we destroy this planet, we destroy it for everyone who lives on it, including them, so it is in everyone's interest that we do as good a job as we can, and encourage others to join us before it's too late.

CHAPTER 5

BEST WAY TO HELP ANIMALS

"The purpose of human life is to serve, and to show compassion and the will to help others."

- Albert Schweitzer

What is the best way to help animals? The first thing that comes to my mind is to simply stop eating them! This has a huge impact on the number of animals killed every year and the more people that go vegan, the fewer animals are killed. Over 60 billion farmed animals are killed every year on land and in the oceans, it tops a trillion lives. If we can get the vegan population from 1% to 10%, imagine how fewer animals will have to die just to satisfy peoples habits, taste, convenience, and tradition?

When we started our Epic Animal Quest, we asked ourselves what we could do to help the most animals. Our mission with our Quest is to travel the world working with animal sanctuaries and shelters and directly with animals that need our help. This is awesome, but we can help more animals by assisting other people to make the connection and go Vegan. So we planned to lead by example and promote compassion through action and share our stories, experiences, and information with as many people as possible. If we can encourage people not to eat animals or use animal related products, then we can quite literally save thousands of lives and reduce the unnecessary suffering of thousands of sentient beings. If we can then encourage those people to encourage more people to do the same, then things can change quickly and dramatically.

We can all stop eating animals, and it is something most people in the world can choose to do immediately. So what is holding them back? Unfortunately, eating meat comes with a long history of habit, tradition, convenience, and taste. Breaking habits can be difficult, especially if the person has no desire to do so, but don't give up hope, information is power and armed with the right information it is possible to show people the importance of going vegan.

So if the answer is to stop eating animals, how can we encourage more people to do just that? Well, that's why I wrote my book The Vegan Argument: Why there really is an

answer for everything. It's about helping people to understand why vegans choose the vegan lifestyle and why it is better for the animals, the planet, and our health. It's about
showing how eating, wearing, exploiting, and abusing animals is morally unjustifiable and providing all the answers to
most of the objections against Veganism. We can then use
that information in our activism and change people's minds.

I strongly believe that we should never advocate for a
slow 'transition' or 'journey' from Carnism to Veganism.
Some people will take this approach, and we can encourage
their Vegan choices along the way, but we should be focused
on a complete switch to a vegan lifestyle and really stress that
Veganism is not just about diet but about a complete lifestyle
and philosophy of living. So I work for a swift switch to Veganism and then offer as much help and support as possible.

When doing this, I like to remember how I went Vegan. I
arrived at Veganism on my own without meeting anyone or
being the target of any activism. While I was looking at what
I could do to make the world a better place and improve the
future for my children, I read books on compassion by Karen
Armstrong. Her words and YouTube speeches resonated with
me like nothing before, but she always talked about compassion with only humans in mind. I knew that if I was to really
live a compassionate life, I had to show compassion for all
beings, at all times, and in all places.

As I started to think about this and research how to show compassion for animals, I came across Gary Yourofsky, then Earthlings, and after watching the Earthlings Documentary I literally went Vegan overnight. I researched, and fact-checked, and found almost every detail was true and within a week, my wife Rachael and our two children were Vegan too. Shortly after, we set up our Epic Animal Quest and changed our lives completely. We are certainly not unique, and I have learned that many people come to Veganism through Gary Yourofsky, Earthlings, James Aspey, and many other Vegan activists. Our story is quite typical, but often there will be someone who starts the ball rolling. We can all be that person who sows the seed in someone's mind and sets them off to discover the truth, make the connection, and go Vegan.

So I strongly believe that the best way to help animals is first to choose not to eat or exploit them, and then to encourage other people to do the same. How we do this is going to depend on our own individual personalities and skills. My family and I work directly with animals around the world so we are doing hands-on work that we can share with everyone through our platforms. We write a blog (posting daily) and write books, create memes, cartoons, and merchandise, all aimed at promoting Veganism and encouraging others to adopt the Vegan lifestyle. We like to promote the positive side of Veganism while writing about thought-provoking topics around animal ethics.

Think about what skills you have and how you can apply them to animal activism. If you are a writer, then perfect, write books, blogs, articles, memes, and as many other ideas as you can think of. If you are an artist, a videographer, photographer, musician, life coach, fitness coach, or are experienced in any other field, then use that and incorporate Veganism into what you do.

Individuals can make an immediate difference just by making the connection and deciding to not eat animals or use animals for entertainment, experimentation, clothing, or profit. As more and more individuals come together, we find ourselves in a position where we truly can change the world for the better. When we start to get active in activism, we can make these changes even bigger. We can go even further by using our professions, expertise, and time to make changes we would never have thought possible. Sometimes, it only takes one idea to change the world, and it could be yours!

CHAPTER 6

ONE PERSON CAN MAKE A DIFFERENCE

"Each one of us can make a difference. Together we make change."

- Barbara Mikulski

"The love of all living creatures is the most noble attribute of man."

- Charles Darwin

One person can make a difference, but together, we can change the world. I truly believe this. We have seen it in the past so many times. Minorities are ridiculed, oppressed, and ignored, but over time, as their numbers grow, the minorities can impact the majority, and eventually become the majority. One person deciding never to eat meat, eggs, or dairy ever again has an immediate effect on the market. It may be minuscule, but every time someone stops buying something, the demand for that thing is reduced. If I stop buying meat, eggs, dairy, and fish, and my family does too, then that is a considerable amount; especially if you add it up over a month, a year, or lifetime. Now, what if I can help 10 people, 100 people, 1000 people, maybe 10,000 people see the benefits of the vegan lifestyle through activism? What if they get involved in activism, and each goes on to help 1,000 other people too? Now we start to see a very real difference on the horizon, and we can certainly imagine the sun rising on a Vegan world.

Gary Yourofsky, the famous animal rights activist who toured the US giving lectures to high school students, took a trip to Israel. Since his visit, the number of vegans in Israel has skyrocketed, and it is the fastest growing vegan population in the world. Gary's words helped to show them the truth, and he has made a massive stride forward for the animals. The dairy industry in Israel has been, and they have started to offer a wide range of dairy-free alternatives. The demand for dairy decreased, and the demand for vegan alternatives increased. The market saw this and responded with what the customers wanted. This is capitalism at work, so you see we can use it in our favour.

In the UK, a large supermarket chain, Sainsbury's, released a number of vegan cheese products in most of their biggest stores. They saw the demand for vegan alternatives was growing, and they responded not by trying to stop it or distract it, but by providing exactly what the customers wanted. There are stories like this in supermarkets all over the world. When the truth is put in the right hands, amazing changes can happen.

Just because it may seem like there aren't enough of us ve-gans to make a difference, do not be deceived. Veganism is the fastest growing social justice group in the world, and we are making things happen. More people are getting it, mak-ing the connection, and the momentum is building; and building fast. This is al because or activism that we can join in on! Even if there weren't enough vegans to make a differ-ence, what kind of people would we be if we just went along with the crowd knowing that that crowd was doing things that we just can't justify morally?

The vegan ocean is made up of single drops of defiance. Single drops of change that continue to build up every day, over many years. Given enough time, this ocean will rise, and the waves of change will crash against the societal rocks and eventually, little by little, meat consumption could very well be just a distant echo in a discarded shell.

CHAPTER 7

INSULTS & OPPOSITION

"Never argue with an idiot."

- George Carlin

Following a blog post we wrote about compassionless dairy farming in a US owned Dairy Farm in Cambodia, we started to receive some weird messages, hate, and negativity. This made it very real to us that what we were doing when we were filming and writing about animals who we met, was actually affecting the humans who were exploiting them. We met them face to face, and we exposed their cruelty. It doesn't feel nice to write something that has an effect on someone's life, of course, it doesn't, but it is far worse for us to see the exploitative and abusive treatment of animals and not say anything at all. It's also not nice to be insulted. But a few hurt feelings is the price we sometimes have to pay if we really want to speak up for animals and try our best to affect change. Facing the people who are involved in the animal industries is where the theory gets very real, and the first few times it happens, it can be uncomfortable. But it is our duty to stand up for these animals and as Alice Walker said, "Activism is my rent for living on this planet."

We have debated farmers before, chefs, and other people involved in animal industries, but the dairy farm post was the first time we stood out and actually confronted people we knew and who knew us. The backlash was not pleasant, but no one corrected us on the information we put across. Instead, they brought up tired old arguments like Monsanto, Soybean destruction, general vegan derogatory statements, accused us of attention seeking and having an agenda, insulted us, and the worst of all insulted our children. We can easily address the Monsanto, soybean, and vegan arguments and show how they are heavily linked to the meat and dairy industries, but how do we deal with personal insults and attempts to assassinate our characters? How do we deal with insults against our children? Simple, we either ignore them or use the insults to show who we are dealing with and write about it! What about being called attention seekers with an agenda? To this, I say thank you for the compliment!

Obviously, any organisation, cause, business, charity or social enterprise needs attention. Marketing 101 is to find and utilise the most underpriced attention! Anyone in business knows this. The dairy industry has been an expert in marketing for decades, but having been confronted with social media for the last 10 or so years, they have been presented with a fight they are losing. When people in society are given both sides of a story, and the means to fact check for themselves and then make their own informed decisions, change can happen. It can happen fast and in a huge way. That's where we fit in. We do our small bit to counter all the misleading information and marketing used by the Dairy industry and add what we find to the pool of Vegan animal activists who are working every day for the animals.

We certainly don't deny wanting attention, and we definitely want more of it; we haven't even started yet! Attention is the gateway to change! We use our lifestyle and as many ways as we can think of to gain attention and direct it towards animal abuse, mistreatment, and exploitation and all the ways we can all avoid it. We have devoted our lives to this and will never be ashamed of asking for attention for an injustice that we are so passionate about standing up for and changing.

One thing that crops up time and time again is the accusation that we have an agenda, and I am sure you are going to be accused of it too. It is usually framed in a way that suggests that an agenda is a bad thing to have. We all know the agenda behind the dairy industry; get people to drink and consume as much dairy as possible and use government grants, subsidies, false advertising, misleading information, and clever marketing to do it. Make out something that is harmful to us is actually good for us, and then sell as much of it as possible for the highest price they can. Lobby governments on animal welfare regulations so they can cut corners and reduce costs in the farms and watch the profits go up.

We are very proud of our own agenda and have developed it consciously. We encourage and help people to Go Vegan, Stay Vegan, and Get Active in Activism. So to be told we have an agenda and have a stranger identify what it is is something we actually take as a compliment! Without an agenda, how can we clearly define our goals and work out roadmaps to achieve them? If we want to make a change in anything we do, we have to identify the problems and the injustices and work out ways to tackle them. Part of that planning process is to develop an agenda, an idea of the outcomes we want to achieve.

Of course, our agenda will not be in line with the Dairy industries agenda (and their oddly loyal supporters who fear their wittle milkshakes will be taken away from them) and it can't be if we want to change it. This is where the friction develops between staunch supporters of this cruel industry and compassionate people who look to go dairy free and

choose alternatives that are better for the animals, their
health, their children health, and our planet.

Going up against large and powerful industries like the
dairy industry is never going to be smooth or easy. With so
many people consuming and loving dairy products, our criticism of dairy can often be taken as a criticism of their lifestyle; which I suppose indirectly it is. But while we don't go
out with intent to cause offence or upset anyone, we won't let
the risk of people taking offence stop us telling the truth and
showing what is really happening to the animals, our health,
and our planet because of our demand for dairy products.
Why should we keep quiet just because a few people will take
offence? After all, we don't give offence, it is taken, and that
is out of our control.

We don't name workers, and we don't attack people personally or insult them and their family or use intimidating
words to threaten or lambast. We are in no way aggressive in
our approach and only use the facts and our interpretation
of them based on what we have seen, heard, smelled, and
touched. Our pieces are opinion pieces based on our experience in the world and nothing more.

What kind of people would we be if we insulted the
children of the people who we feel are responsible for animal
cruelty? That would make us complete scum bags in my
opinion, and if we had to resort to insulting peoples children,

then I guess we would have no facts to make our counter arguments with and admit defeat. Insulting children in a serious debate on the welfare and treatment of animals is a disgrace. It also reveals who we are dealing with, though. Any time we get insults like these, we won't engage with them. A debate or argument is something we will get into but like we said earlier, trolls belong under the bridge, and we leave them there to throw their mud and tantrums.

We were told by a worker on a public Facebook post that we were more 'worthless than all the bull calves in dairy farming. It's so funny.' [Insert laughing rotating heads here]. This comment made our point for us. The animals are mere commodities, and the baby boy calves are worthless to an industry that focusses on profits and ignores pain. So while it is not nice to be insulted, and certainly not nice to hear our children being insulted, it is nice to have our points made for us by the people whose agenda is so unaligned to our own.

Our approach isn't to insult and damage people and businesses, our agenda is much more than that. We focus on the supply and demand and try to influence the demand away from things that are cruel and unnecessary and towards things that are cruelty-free (or as much as they can be) and ethical. In short, we basically show what is happening, state why we don't agree with it because of x y and z, and if you don't agree with it either, we encourage you to try other products instead. We don't need to insult, make things up, intimidate or name call; the truth is enough to shock people into action, and if we had to resort to these tactics, then I think we would have lost already.

We don't ask people to leave a country and 'go back to their own country', and we don't go through their profiles and information to try and come across as some super sleuth who can name them and identify things about them and their past (even though we wholeheartedly are public about who we are and what we do because we have no shame and are proud of our lifestyle). We admit our failings and openly state very frequently that we were guilty of all the things we are now against for most of our lives. We know we are hypocrites but don't pretend that we are otherwise. We don't attack the attackers, we attack the foundations by which their cruelty and animal abuse are based on.

I would like to thank all the people who made negative comments because they not only revealed who we are dealing with and strengthened some of our arguments, but they gave me a subject to write about which is something I love to do. Often, Vegan activists are seen as the underdogs, and I don't mind that. Being the underdog is dangerous; we may get kicked from time to time, but we also have the ability to bite back.

CHAPTER 8

BE INSPIRED

"Bigger isn't better. Better is better."

- Unknown

As with most things in life, inspiration is often needed to help us to get up and get active. Vegan activism is a great way to take action against injustice and to do something you are passionate about to make a positive change in the world. However, there are days when even the best of us want to hit that snooze button and curl up for more sleep rather than get up early on our day off and go out in the rain and cold to stand vigil at a slaughterhouse or join a Vegan outreach event. So this chapter is all about some resources to keep you on point and to help you remind yourself why we are doing this and who we are doing this for. When I need some motivation, I look to a speech by someone like James Aspey, or I remember some undercover footage I took, and then I soon forget that extra nine minutes of sleep!

I thought it would be useful to break down this chapter into sections with some awesome documentaries, books, speeches, YouTube channels, websites, and other resources so that when you need something to get you going, the answers are just a click away. Of course, there are free copies of many of these online, but we can't recommend this here. Buying the products also helps contribute to the activists who made them, so if you are in a position to and want to purchase, everyone wins. Thank you.

Documentaries

Watch Earthlings Here for ethics and animal rights http://www.nationearth.com/earthlings-1/

Watch Blackfish Here for ethics http://blackfishmovie.com

Watch What The Health here for your health http://www.whatthehealthfilm.com

Watch Forks over Knives here for your health https://www.forksoverknives.com

Watch Vegucated here for your health http://www.getvegucated.com

Watch Cowspiracy here for the Environment http://www.cowspiracy.com

Watch Sharkwater here for the environment http://www.sharkwater.com

Books

Read Animal Liberation for ethics
Read How Not To Die for your health
Read The China Study for your health
Read Farmageddon for the Environment
Read my book The Vegan Argument for why Veganism is the answer

YouTube Channels

Gary Yourofsky on YouTube for all things Vegan
James Aspey for a great approach and introduction to Veganism
The Vegan Society Podcast for Vegan news and features
Bite Size Vegan for all things Vegan

Speeches and Lectures

James Aspey
Gary Yourofsky

Websites

VEGANUARY for support on Going Vegan and trying it for one month www.veganuary.com

VIVA for animal issues https://www.viva.org.uk

PETA for news http://www.peta.org

The Vegan Society for all things vegan and the Source of Veganism http://thevegansociety.com

Nutrition Facts for Science and Nutrition http://nutritionfacts.org

CHAPTER 9

ACTIVISM VERSUS CHARITY

"If they are too big to fail, make them smaller."

- George P. Shultz

I've heard it said that charity is activism, but I think that isn't quite true. I think it's important to make the differentiation so this chapter will do just that. Animal rights Activism is usually carried out by individuals involved in groups without leadership and without funding. Often, groups of people will form around an issue that they are all passionate about and they will work in their own spare time using their own money and resources to solve it. A perfect example of animal rights activism is the animal save/ animal vigil movement. Taking vigil and standing together with other vegans at a slaughterhouse is a unique experience that I am grateful to have received.

The people I stood with were there for the animals. They didn't fill in any bids for grants or claim any expenses to get them there, and like me, they paid for their own petrol or train didn't ask for donations so they could use their phones and cameras to film the poor animals and they didn't use the animals as examples of animal abuse to get donations to solve it.

The problems in activism are perhaps long-term problems that can't be solved by money alone. To solve them, it will take people and lots of them! We would have to raise an un-imaginable amount of money to be able to get people to go vegan in vast numbers or to replace the meat products with alternatives. It seems the way to get a high percentage of the population to go vegan is by sharing information and experi-ences and each of us encouraging others to follow and go vegan too. When they go vegan and encourage others to go the numbers will soon rise. This is something we can all do, and it doesn't take much time and can even be free.

Of course, we need money to live, and charities need money to function, but when the primary topic is money (and it usu-ally always is with charity), I get disappointed and discour-aged. When we took part in activism where money wasn't the driving force or the element that was missing to get us together, money was irrelevant. So without money, did we have an impact? The answer is simply yes. We know that people went vegan and took interest in Veganism because we were there speaking out for the animals. Our actions stimu-lated debate, questions, and interest, and showed people that the beef they love so much is not beef but real life cows who were killed when all they wanted to do was live.

Activism in the purest form comes from passion and from acting out of a moral obligation to make a positive change in the world. When the activists don't have to be somewhere like the slaughterhouse and get absolutely nothing from being there, what are their motives? Surely they are there for the animals and nothing else? Surely, they are there for change?

I know I didn't want to go to these hell holes and I didn't want to stand around freezing cold in the rain, watching poor cows being driven into a slaughterhouse, hear them be killed, and then watch their skins be driven along on a forklift truck and their innards and heads be tipped into a skip. It was awful to experience, but if we didn't experience it then no one would know, and no one would have acknowledged those beautiful cows that I was helpless to help. When people get together without any personal motive, amazing things can happen. Passion in these activities and with these groups is far higher than anything I've witnessed in charities, and the people committed and all for the cause.

Do some people gain from being there? There are some famous celebrity vegans now, and I'm told they are sometimes paid to attend some vigils. Does this help the cause? These people are celebrities in the vegan circles, and if you weren't vegan you probably wouldn't have heard of them, so having them there is mostly only going to appeal to vegans. Yes, they are excellent at converting people to Veganism and talking through the points, but no more than many of the other activists I've met. They just have a popular YouTube channel and are maybe more outspoken about the fringe issues.

Paying activists to attend vigils is not something that sits right with me. I can see how they would get paid for their You-Tube channel as it takes some work to make a video a week, but being paid to do something that is at the core of what we do as activists is not cool. I guess this brings us onto Patreon and we should discuss it. Many of these celebrities are funded by other vegans. Now it's up to everyone how they spend their hard earned money. But do the outspoken vegans who it could be argued preach to the converted (I'm guilty of this too) make better use of the money than an animal sanctuary would? When a young you tuber speaks out at a march and makes money for doing so while the people who founded the movement don't get a look in, there seems to be something off to me. When we place individuals as icons of a movement, we disrespect the movement. A movement like Veganism doesn't have or need a leader, and we don't need a spokesperson; we are all spokespeople!

We all need to earn money, and I think we can focus our time and work life on something vegan that benefits other vegans or helps people go vegan or even provide an alternative to non-vegan food. Vegan artists create beautiful artwork for people's homes, I write books around Veganism helping people to go vegan and stay vegan then get active, and other people make informative and entertaining videos about Veganism on YouTube. But getting paid to attend a vigil at a slaughterhouse crosses the line somewhat.

I've recently filmed a slaughterhouse where pigs were killed up to seven hundred per night. I didn't get paid for it, I didn't sell the footage, and I didn't use it to set up a charity so I could get donations to go and film another slaughterhouse or farm. I basically gave it away to a bigger organisation to do something with it and get it in front of more people than I ever could. This was done with two other activists who made nothing out of the endeavour, we all did it for the animals and to make a difference.

When we start thinking that we should be paid to do these things, then we need to question why we are doing them. Money isn't my motivator, and I've made a commitment to live a different life that is based on more than I earn or have. It's based on what I do and how I do it. What legacy I leave behind is super important to me and doing the right thing means more than a cheque ever would.

But why is charity any different? Charities need money; it's the lifeblood of the organisations, and without it, the charities wouldn't exist. Charities often rely on volunteers and have a mix of paid staff and those who volunteer. This isn't bad, but it is different, once you start having paid employees, you start having the same issues you would have in any regular business. Underperformance, lack of experience, bad hiring, inefficiencies, and general differences in staff that you would find in any business or organisation. Some do the minimum amount of work required to keep their job while others do a bit more and very few go the extra mile.

All their wages (or the majority) are paid for by donation and sponsorship from people giving money to solve a problem the charity has adopted and proposed a solution for. Now, this money is being used to pay people to do jobs inefficiently. This can't be helped once organisations grow to a certain size or have intentions to grow. Money is assigned to different things, and then as with any organisation that involves bureaucracy and self-administered red tape that slows things down and then the money will often be wasted or mismanaged.

How many charities do you know have solved a problem and then closed their doors? Perhaps they solved a problem and then moved on to another problem, but can you name any? Compare that with how many charities you know who have millions in donations yet still haven't solved the problem. How many have actually thought up more problems so they can get more money in funding and donations?

These are problems you don't usually see in animal activism and if money is involved, it is usually as part of a fundraiser or GoFundMe where all the money goes to a specific cause, solution, or item of equipment that is needed and I would safely say that the person raising the funds and organising the fundraiser wasn't often paid for doing so. This raises the questions as to who we should donate to for best results? Someone who is paid regardless of success and wouldn't be there if they weren't paid, or someone who works for free and is not motivated by money or personal gain? We are starting to go more into effective altruism here as well as topics I go deep into with our book, Beehive: serve the idea solve the problem. Beehive was written to give an alternative to the outdated charity model based on collaboration and social enterprise. If this subject interests you, I highly recommend having a read.

I can only go my own experience so far, and I know how powerful passionate, like-minded people can be at effective activism. The Charity model is ineffective, and I don't like being a part of the fundraising activities unless it is something I can see working and having a positive effect on specific problems. Beaurocracy will kill any organisation and will distract people from their goals. This can't happen in activism and money can't get in the way. The things that have the biggest impact come about from collaboration and people helping each other to go vegan and stay vegan. If we can help them get active in the activism world too, then we have a chance to do something great here. We can still raise money to help individual campaigns and activities, but when we compare how much time and resources help one Cat or Dog with how many animals one person going vegan saves, the numbers quickly swing towards the vegan dial.

If one vegan saves 400 animals per year, then that is a huge result. What if we help 100, 1000, or 10000 people go vegan? Then we are helping to save thousands of animals and what an incredible result that would be in our lifetime. Then what if those people helped others go vegan? All of a sudden we have actually made a difference and helped change the world for the better and we did together and because of each other. To do this, we don't have to donate to other activists to make videos and talk to the public, and instead, we would be more effective if we spent the money on our own activism.

CHAPTER 10

GRASSROOTS MOVEMENT

"Lack of money is the root of all evil."

- George Bernard Shaw

Since we started Epic Animal Quest, we have frequently come across phrases like 'capacity building', 'grassroots', and 'community action'. We adopted the term 'grassroots community action' when we worked with businesses, social enterprises, activists, and individuals involved in the initiative led by Animal Mama, a Veterinary Clinic and Pet Wellness Centre in Phnom Penh who have adopted the Social Enterprise model to help abandoned, sick and injured street and pagoda animals.

We have also been involved in animal activism activities, and have worked with other individuals to form our own grassroots movements and organised ourselves as individuals to identify problems in our community and do something about them. On top of this, together, we have developed our capacity so as to tackle further problems in the future. This has proved very effective in using few resources and no funding to achieve success in different areas, and when contrasted with the output of other methods, the grassroots movement method can come out on top both in efficiency and effectiveness. The term Grassroots is used by many organisations so we felt it should be explained and explored, and included in this book. But what exactly does it mean to be a 'Grassroots' movement? Let's find out!

There are many definitions, but they all have the same thing in common, which is that they consist of individuals in a community working together to affect change. A grassroots movement will develop organically and is not centred around an organisation with paid directors and employees.

Some organisation and coordination have to take place, and you may see this described as 'grassroots organising'. It's a democratic process that engages people by working in a bottom-up fashion and decisions are made by the whole group. Leaders may emerge organically or out of necessity, but they aren't necessary for a grassroots movement to work. One important thing I love about true grassroots movements is that the people who are part of it are not paid! No one benefits financially, and it is driven by passion rather than profit.

What about astroturfing? This is a really interesting phrase I discovered when writing this post and I guess it's similar to when companies 'greenwash' their business practices. Astroturfing is when an organisation that is driven by cash infusions - this can be from a variety of sources such as donations or coalitions - mimic the grassroots approach.

Unlike true grassroots movements, astroturfers do not engage individual volunteers effectively, and they run a more structured and bureaucratic organisation with paid employees and everyone involved having a job title. There could be an argument that the failure to authentically engage and keep hold of volunteer individuals over time, shows that astroturfing is ineffective and certainly inefficient in affecting real change on the local level, but that's a whole new post!

Any organisation with money can use this astroturfing method in their marketing campaigns, and it can be used in a very manipulative way for them to promote themselves and gain more donations or coalition members. So next time you hear someone say they are a Grassroots movement, just ask them if they are funded by other organisations, do they get paid, and do they have employees? If they answer yes to any of those questions, then perhaps they are astroturfers in disguise!

Astroturfing is a critique we can make on the Save movement. What started out as a true grassroots movement, hs now developed into an organisation based on the charity model. It encourages donations, attends international animal welfare Expos, and pays for unnecessary overheads just like most other charities. Grassroots movements are not reliant on monthly donations, yet animalsave.org states it is a grassroots movement and that it needs monthly and one-off donations to run campaigns. They can't have it both ways. Why donate to them when we could use our money to attend the vigils and run our own campaigns? This may be splitting hairs, but it makes my point that organisations move away from being a movement and adopt an organisational approach the minute they have paid staff and expense accounts or fundraise to attend international animal Expos.

Don't get me wrong, animal save vigils are different from the AnimalSave.org global movement. I believe animal vigils are crucial to make a change, I just want them to stay as a true grassroots movement and feel that there is no requirement for a donation based organisation of paid staff to lead it. Perhaps the organisation has its place, but that may weaken the movement rather than strengthen it.

In this case, it seems the grass really could be greener on the other side, and true grassroots movements are perhaps the most effective and efficient way to affect real lasting change locally and even globally. When we look back at history, changes haven't occurred because one person or organisation demanded it; change has happened over long periods of time because likeminded people have identified a problem and banded together to do something about it. They refused to stand by and watch injustice, manipulation, and oppression take over, and they stood together to fight it.

CHAPTER 11

COMPASSION FOR ALL

"If you want others to be happy, practice compassion. If you want to be happy, practice compassion."

- Dalai Lama

I decided to include this chapter in the book to give you an idea of how we became Vegan as a family. It was all because of compassion, and I believe that if we can spread compassion and challenge people to understand what it means to be compassionate, then we can make great progress in our activism. Change has to come from ourselves, and we have to make our own decision to change. If we can use compassion to help people to make their own decision to go Vegan, then we have to focus on it a lot during our animal activism.

Since we had children, I have been thinking about what I can do to make their future better. With war and destruction going on every day all around the world, I was starting to think their future looked bleak. I looked at all the major threats to the planet - and our humanity - but struggled to see what could I do to stop war, terrorism, and famine?

During my research into an article I was writing on religion, way before we started Epic Animal Quest, I interviewed a number of religious people including our local village Vicar. The three hours I spent with the Vicar sent me on a direction I never imagined I would go in. After talking, he recommended a writer called Karen Armstrong. He seemed to think I was on some kind of 'quest' and felt Karen Armstrong would help me answer some of the questions I had. Now, I am not a religious man and if I had to, I would describe myself as anti-theist. I am not a believer in any kind of 'woo-woo' either, but I felt something strange that day that is difficult to describe. I felt like everything around me changed, almost like the pieces of my reality had been rearranged. Like a door had been unlocked or a crack appeared, and I had to walk through it. I know this sounds silly, but I felt it and decided to go along for the ride!

I went away from the meeting and looked up Karen Armstrong on YouTube that night. Amongst a variety of topics, I found some speeches she had given on compassion.

Immediately I connected with everything she was saying. It was as if she had read my mind and was giving me all the answers and solutions I needed. Compassion was the answer I had been looking for all this time. Right away I knew I had to live a compassionate life and to do it, I needed to change everything. But if I wanted to change the world, I first had to change myself.

For the next week, I listened to her speeches on the way to work and on the way home. I thought about it during the day and couldn't believe I had found someone that resonated with me so clearly. In all the speeches, the emphasis was always on showing compassion to humans, but my thoughts went to the other animals. Why should we only show compassion to the human animal? Surely all living sentient beings deserved the same display of love, kindness, and compassion?

This is where I made the first step away from my old life and forward to my new one. If I was to lead a truly compassionate life, then I needed to show compassion to all animals. I started to look at animal rights, and for the next couple of weeks, I immersed myself in the world of Veganism. I consumed every resource I could, reading, watching, and listening to as much information as possible. It felt like I was slowly being woken up from a dream and brought back into a reality I didn't recognise. How could I not have known the extent of the cruelty, abuse, torture, and murder that humans inflict on other animals every second of every day?

This wasn't just about me. My wife Rachael and our children were involved too. During our research, one of the biggest impacts on my family and me was the Earthlings Documentary. After two weeks of reading and learning about Veganism, my wife, my 9-year-old daughter and I all sat down to watch it. We decided that my 5-year-old boy was too young, so once he was asleep, we put it on to watch. We were all in tears by the end of the documentary. Everything I had read about and listened to was put together into a 2-hour documentary that graphically revealed the truth behind meat, fish, eggs, dairy, clothes, entertainment, and pretty much every aspect of our lives. It played out like a horror movie, but sadly, this wasn't make-believe, this was real life.

That was it for us. We knew immediately that we had to Go Vegan and we had to change our lifestyle completely. How could we have been part of this for so long? I was 37 at the time, and Rachael was 45. All our lives we had consumed the abuse, imprisonment, enslavement, torture, and death of all these animals. The guilt we felt was overwhelming, but it fuelled us on to make some decisions that would change our lives forever.

Within a month, I had created Epic Animal Quest, built the website, and set in motion our new social enterprise. We started to make plans to leave our old lives behind and embark on our new compassionate ones. Now we knew better, we had no choice but to do better. Now, 2 years later, we find ourselves slowly travelling around the world working with animals and people we meet who are involved in animal rights. We have sold almost everything we own, sold our business (we pretty much gave it away), and left the UK to work with animal shelters and sanctuaries in every country we visit. Finally, we are doing something that can make the world a better place. We can actually make a difference and leave this world better than we found it and it's all because of finding compassion.

What exactly is compassion? Compassion is described in the Charter as treating others as you would wish to be treated yourself. This 'Golden Rule' has been at the centre of many religions throughout history, but it has been muddied by the abuse of doctrines and dogma. Compassion isn't just an idea, but a way of life and it should be given at all times, to all beings, in all places. The Charter for Compassion only includes human beings, not other animals, so it is not the world-changing solution we need. Of course, we should be compassionate to our fellow humans, but we should not forget that the animals are sentient beings too. They have emotions, they love, and they grieve just like we do. Animals feel fear and suffer in ways we could never imagine; all at the hands of humans.

If we can take steps to stop hurting and killing animals, then surely we would stop hurting and killing ourselves too? The first step is to put ourselves in the place of the being who is suffering. Would we want to be separated from our mother at birth? Would we want to have our beaks, tails, or testicles cut off? Would we want to be killed so others could eat us just because they like the way we taste? Would we want to be forcibly impregnated so we could keep being milked for other animals to drink? Would we want to be torn from our family and kept in a small tank to entertain other animals? Would we want to be skinned or plucked alive just to keep others warm or 'en vogue'? The answer to all of these questions is obviously no. So why is it ok for us to do it to others? If we want to be compassionate people, then we have to stop doing all of these things to the animals, and we have to live in congruence with our self-construct. We have to start living by the Golden Rule and applying it to all living beings.

Once we knew better, we were obligated to do better, and if we can help others in any way, then just have to. If we want our children to grow up in a world that is safe and healthy, then we all have to act now. I fear that if we don't, then they will not have any kind of future at all.

We really can change this world for the better. At one time I didn't think we could, but now I know we can. All around the world, people are waking up and realising that we can't carry on like this. Starting with our own lives, we can show compassion for all beings, we can help other beings, and we can change our own destructive behaviours. Once we have changed, we can help others to do the same. We can help others to know better and hope they will choose to do better too. Together, we can make this world a better place than we found it.

I have often written about the quote by Horace Mann, 'Be ashamed to die until you have won some victory for humanity.' This idea has been with me for the last 10 years, and now I feel that if I can achieve the goals we set out in our Epic Animal Quest, then my time here would not have been wasted. This victory could be a moral one, and we could choose to show that humanity is not about dominance, greed, and destruction, but instead about love, kindness, and compassion for all.

SECTION 2

GET ACTIVE IN ANIMAL ACTIVISM

CHAPTER 12

TALK ABOUT VEGANISM

"Is awareness really the problem?"

- Seth Godin

Vegan Activism Talk About Veganism

This isn't Fight Club, this is Vegan Club, so tell everyone about it! We should never be ashamed to speak about Veganism and why we passionately choose to be Vegan. Talking about Veganism is really easy to do, and includes social media, so anytime we have a few minutes spare, we can post a talking point or join in on another conversation. As we all know, we do often get ridiculed, dismissed, and are even shown anger and disdain from some people, but that should never stop us. We can, after all, change the subject or walk away if things get uncomfortable, or at the very least, block people on social media or simply leave the conversation.

I have been in a few conversions that end in the other person becoming really flustered and often angry, but it isn't always like that. We can converse with our friends, loved ones, and colleagues without it always resulting in a fight or argument like this. When we first went Vegan, we were much more argumentative as we couldn't believe the things that went on and we reacted to our own ignorance by trying to let everyone know what we discovered. We soon found that arguing with people didn't get us anywhere, and then we came across James Aspey. He has a brilliant manner to him, and when he talks with people about Veganism, he manages to get all the information and points across in a friendly way that is not confrontational at all. Of course, some people still manage to take offence, but that will happen with pretty much any subject that people disagree on.

People today get too easily offended by the truth and have this idea that their own beliefs are more important than the facts. We should hold no respect for someones erroneous beliefs and should not be put off from sharing the truth just in case someone takes offence. This is a subtle but important point; we don't give offence, people choose to take it. How is telling the truth a bad thing, especially when real lives (60 billion a year to be precise) are at stake?

One way that we have found to keep things civil is not to judge people, or at least not judge them to their face, haha! I think we are all very guilty of judging others and their behaviour and for a subject as important as animal rights, it is difficult to not come across as judgemental, as the decision to follow the vegan lifestyle is in itself a judgement on society; there's no getting around that. But judgements don't have to be negative. We can point out that yes, it is terrible what is happening to the animals, but look at the all the amazing benefits that the vegan lifestyle offers!

We were all probably meat eaters at one time and thought the same as everyone else, and this is important to remember. How would we feel if someone randomly stopped us in the street and started lecturing us about our lifestyle? Immediately we would retract and get defensive, so the conversational approach has to be the best way to get people talking and thinking about Veganism. It is easy to speak in the manner of someone like Gary Yourofsky, but we forget that when he was talking in his confrontational and unique approach, it wasn't during a conversation but rather during a lecture or a speech in a college or other organisation. When it's rhetorical like that, then we have more freedom to be confrontational and use shock tactics to get our points across, but doing that in a one on one environment is just not as effective.

This doesn't mean we have to go easy on people where the truth is concerned, though and remember it's not our point of view or our 'belief'; the truth is the truth. Once we have told them all the information about how badly animals are treated and how extreme the mass killings are, we would expect them to at the very least think about it all and then hopefully go on to do something about it and change their own lifestyle. If they don't, then what kind of person does that make them? This is precisely where the frustration and anger experienced by both parties are born. Many people don't want to change, and they don't like you pointing out that what they are doing is terrible. So how to get over this? I suggest we remain dogged in our approach. We keep consistent, persistent, and positive and don't forget to inject some humour because after all, losing our desire to eat dead animals, doesn't mean we have to lose our sense of humour too!

If you are at work, perhaps you could just talk about your delicious lunch you have made. If someone is talking about losing weight (and so many people do, especially in the New Year) then perhaps offer to help them with a few suggestions for healthy meals and snacks. When they see you looking great and always being healthy, they will want to have what you have. Over time you can start adding more and more information about animal cruelty into the conversation as well as the benefits to the environment and health. You don't have to stand up and give a one-hour presentation or deliver monograms every day, just be normal, be yourself and talk about Animal Rights in a calm and thought-provoking way.

One thing you will find when you start talking about Veganism is that you will be hit with the same few objections. Protein, B12, child abuse, unhealthy, expensive, you just eat lettuce, plants are alive too, and the infamous lions tho', these are all the common ones. It will help you dramatically to have prepared for these and have tried and tested answers to hand. That's why I wrote my book 'The Vegan Argument: Why there really is an answer for everything.' I detail close to one hundred objections against Veganism and answer them in a normal conversational way. I have also written many blog posts about objections to Veganism so have a read and join in the conversation too.

When someone brings up an objection, and you can confidently and correctly handle it, then every other objection they bring up too, then you show them immediately that the general perception of Veganism is totally wrong. You also show them that the information they have believed for most of their lives is just not true. This can be a very powerful wake-up call and all through a few simple conversations.

Although it sucks to realise it - especially when we first go Vegan - many people just don't want to talk about Veganism and will be totally convinced by everything that they have always believed throughout their lives. Even when we have shown footage of slaughterhouse treatment of animals, talked about health benefits, and offered sound arguments that eating meat negatively affects our the land, oceans, and the entire planet, people will still rather eat dead animals and their products than not eat them. Even when we show the many alternatives to food, cleaning products, clothes, and entertainment, some people will not be at all interested. I've shown people undercover footage of slaughterhouses that I took myself, and they still didn't believe it; or more precisely, they chose not to.

Is it our fault that they don't want to listen or change when they do? Of course, we have to take responsibility and realise that we are not as good at talking about Veganism as people like James Aspey, but the facts are the facts, and the truth is the truth. If people who eat animals and their products won't accept the facts and truth even after they know how cruel and destructive their lifestyle choice (and it is a choice) is, then there are limits to what we can do. If people say to us that, yes it is cruel and we don't need to eat or use any animal products to survive, thrive, and live an awesome life, but feel they can't live without cheese or bacon and would rather eat those things than stop paying for the cruelty, then we will hit a dead end. We can keep drip feeding information and continue to be a presence to remind them there is another more compassionate way to live. Perhaps we can focus more on the people who do show an interest and do take on the truth and then feel a need and desire to do something about the new things they have learned. We can help these people to go Vegan and most importantly, stay Vegan.

People are all different and respond to things in different ways. My Dad gets very irate and just won't talk to me about Veganism, and both of my parents refuse to watch anything related to the dead animal flesh they eat. They would rather not know and carry on in ignorant bliss. It's frustrating that the people closest to me don't want to hear what I am passionate about and that I can't even converse with them normally about it, but this is not unique to my family and me. Often, those people that are closest to us are the hardest to reach. Other people will listen and watch but still eat animals and their products regardless. Some will listen and take on the information and change their ways. I guess our job is to find the best way to get to be able to converse with people and get them to see the reality of the meat, egg and dairy industries as well as the misuse of animals in clothing, makeup, hygiene, and entertainment. Once we show them, they will have to think about what they've seen and heard and hopefully act on it.

There are there main areas that people will react and respond to. These are the environment, health, and ethics. If we can find each persons 'hot spot' and talk about issues that will resonate with them, then we have more chance of making a difference for the animals with each of them. Some people just aren't bothered about how the animals suffer (unless they are dogs and then they are more passionate than the most passionate and militant Vegans), but their own health is important to them. Health for some people is just not an issue, but show them a pig being clubbed to death with a metal pole in Asia and they might think that pork is not for them anymore. The environment is perhaps the furthest from us personally, but it still is important to some people. Environmentalist and conservationists are one of the weirdest groups for me. They can be so passionate about saving one particular animal in one specific location, but they are happy to eat twenty other kinds of animals even when they know that eating those animals is one of the biggest contributors to the loss of land and the destruction of our oceans. These can be the most difficult to reason with, but we have to try.

Talking to people in person or online is the best way to get people into Veganism and to open them up to the information that we should all know and be taught about. But there are many ways to use activism to get the message across and in front of the eyeballs of the people who need it. If we take a few of these approaches and attend vigils at slaughterhouses regularly, write articles and share information online, drop off some flyers, and live a positive Vegan lifestyle and share that lifestyle so that others can see how easy and awesome Veganism is, then we have a much better chance of making a positive difference in the world and helping the animals.

So if you take nothing else from this book, make a pledge to talk more about Veganism. I hope this book encourages you to try out some new forms of activism and even join an animal rights group in your area. If there isn't one, then start one! We did in Phnom Penh, and admittedly, there were only two of us so, but it only takes a tiny amount of passionate people to change things, and we made an impact with what we did. Small actions can affect hundreds, even thousands of people and can inspire them to make a change in their life for the animals. So let's get active and look at some of the main forms of Activism we can use to make a difference.

CHAPTER 13

LEAFLETING

"Talk to people no one else is talking to."

- Pete Cashmore

Leaflet dropping and handing out flyers in the street is something that shouldn't be underestimated. It serves as a great way to stop and talk to people and start a conversation about Veganism and animal rights. People who would never ordinarily have a vegan conversation, will stop and talk to you. I found during an earthlings experience in the UK, that people are generally open to hearing what you have to say and pose some interesting (and most often, repetitive) questions. When they leave and take the leaflet with them, there is no doubt that when they get home and unpack their shopping, they might look at the leaflet again and think over the topics that were talked about and discussed. The topics will have an effect on them, and we know this ourselves from meeting an activist in Sydney, Australia when we were younger who told us about how the chickens have their beaks cut off, so they don't peck each other when in such close environments. We stopped eating KFC for about six months but ridiculously still are chicken elsewhere. It is interesting looking back at our behaviour, and at the time we didn't have the internet to go and see footage like we can today, and we didn't take a flyer. Had we taken a flyer and then followed up and visited the website and then explored further, perhaps we would have made a connection much sooner than we did. We still talk about this experience today some 15 years later, so don't underestimate how powerful talking and leafleting actually is; even though it didn't quite work on us at that time.

You don't have to even go into the street and give out leaflets and talk to people. This is not for everyone, and some people just don't feel comfortable talking about Veganism and being challenged. So, instead, order a bunch of leaflets or even design and print your own and then go out and post them through people's letterboxes. It doesn't get less social than this, and if anyone challenges you, you could say you are paid to do it and then don't get involved in the conversation. Or, if you are happy to, use these experiences to talk to people, which if you are cool with, is highly recommended and an awesome way to speak up for the animals and meet people you may never ordinarily meet. I have been pleasantly surprised by how nice people can be and how open they are for you to talk and interact with them. But, once you start telling them how they should behave and act, that's when you can possibly run into problems, and people can get angry. We can't lecture people we've just met, and it has to be a conversation or even a debate if we are to make progress.

We used to have our own shop, and we would leave some leaflets on our counter. People asked about them and took them, and they often started a conversation. It's interesting how sometimes just a small trigger can start someone on a journey in the vegan world and ideals. For me personally, I read a book that wasn't even related directly to Veganism, and that started me into looking into animal rights and Veganism.

A couple of experiences of leafleting stand out to me. I spoke to a lady in the street who was a vegetarian, she had been for many years and if I remember rightly, over a decade. She loved eggs and thought that Vegetarian was enough for the animals. I was vegetarian for a couple of years myself and felt the same way, I thought I was a hero! Anyway, we got talking about eggs, and how the male chicks are separated at hatching and within a short time, they are killed in gruesome ways such as being gassed, suffocated in large plastic bags by the hundreds, or being ground up alive in a crude mincing machine. When I first saw this, I just couldn't believe it happened and had been for so long. This lady couldn't believe it either, and within a few minutes, I watched her go from a confident lady steadfast in her views to someone who was suffering from obvious sadness and disbelief. She took a flyer and agreed to go and look into this further, and I hope she is no longer eating eggs.

Some people are triggered by health, environment, or ethics and animal cruelty. We have found that everyone has their own trigger, and that to be effective, we have to find out and work out what that trigger is. Once we do, we can use the angle that suits them the best. Many people will just forget about the animals and not make the connection, just like we did in Sydney. But if you can get them to take a flyer that gives links so that they can see the proof for themselves, then that could be enough. You could also explain that their health is at risk, and then they may act accordingly based on that information. The environment is another strong trigger for certain people. But, we find that the environment is not the best reason to go vegan and certainly not the best reasons to stay vegan for many people. When it's our health, we can easily cheat ourselves to believe that the stakes are not that high. But when we think of the animals and realise that their deaths and suffering are directly on our hands, eating a sneaky 'bit of cheese' of a bar of chocolate suddenly has more attached to it. Eating that chocolate means that we've contributed to animal cruelty and suffering, it can't be denied, and when more people realise that, they will be compelled to change.

It all sounds great, but how do we know if leafleting works? A 'Leafleting Effectiveness' study was conducted by www.veganoureach.org in 2015, and you can read it here https://veganoutreach.org/les-fall-2016/ As this study was conducted on college campuses, it can not be extrapolated to everyone who received a leaflet, but it does show that giving leaflets and talking to people about Veganism does have a positive impact. They suggest that viewing videos of slaughterhouse footage is also effective. They did not include any data on outreach that focuses on giving Vegan food tasters, but leafleting (and footage if anyone wants to see it) will be part of many events and can only strengthen them.

Although anecdotes are flakey, we can use them to gauge how people react to hearing about the new information and how many actually act on it. When talking to people during outreach or leafletting, some react very strongly, and we have seen people visibly shaken up by viewing the videos, and some even crying. It's no surprise because the footage can be very shocking, especially when we have never really considered what goes on behind the closed slaughterhouse doors in the process of 'humane' slaughter. We have only been to a few outreach events so far, and back in Cornwall, UK, we saw many people respond positively to the outreach and the slaughterhouse vigils. During outreach, people who our group spoke to actually joined us some weeks later and became part of the activist group!

We have seen people take the information and act on it, whether that be a reduction in consumption, elimination of certain products, or a complete commitment to the Vegan lifestyle. Social media allows us to keep in touch and follow up so that we can further assist the transition and help in any way we can. Even if our efforts only make one person go away and think about the issues enough to follow up and research for themselves, then it is worth it. If each person taking part in the outreach can help one person make the connection, then we have to do it. The more people that do this, the more people will go Vegan, and the more animals will be spared a cruel existence and an unnecessary death.

There are a few charities in the UK who you can order flyers from, and Viva.org is a good one to start with.

CHAPTER 14

DISRUPTING

"There's nothing more fundamentally disruptive to the status quo than a new reality."

- Umair Haque

Disrupting is something that we all do quietly or loudly, and if we live or visit areas where animals are being exploited for entertainment and tourism, disrupting is a good activism choice.

Gathering advertising leaflets from places like sea world, circuses, and general animal abusers who front as attractions is pretty easy. We can take their leaflets from different outlets like tourist information spots and hotel foyers, and then take them to be destroyed and recycled and help force awareness down about them. This is simple to do and can take just a little time. Once the animal abusers see the flyers have gone, they may print more, so with a little upkeep, we can keep going around and getting them all. Printing is not a huge expense but it an expense none the less, and distribution is a job they have to keep on top of. If we can force costs up and make these attractions less profitable, then the negative effect will harm them.

Of course, the animals could suffer the consequences so we should attack from a number of angles. If we want to close down a circus, then we could work with a local animal organisation to check and offer medical care for the circus animals. If we are very brave and can do it safely, we could rescue abused animals and work with a shelter to home them and care for them. We disrupt on the one hand and offer care and alternatives with the other. This two-pronged attack will cause damage and offer solutions at the same time. We can also distribute and replace the flyers we remove with those from an ethical tourist business or attraction, so we are in line with the Vegan principle of disrupting the bad and promoting the good.

Vigils are not disruptive but can have an effect on business. If people start realising that it's animal flesh and not meat that they are eating, and they meet their meat through photos and videos at vigils, then connections can be made, and business will be disrupted. Standing vigil outside of an attraction like Sea World is a good way to get attention to a cause or problem, but we have to do it on public property.

We see all too often how important it is to raise awareness about things around the world like Sea World but most of the time that awareness is converted into cash. Activism has the opposite effect and goal. We want to protest outside Sea

World to stop people from going there and spending their money there. We don't want their money or money from anyone whose awareness we are raising. We just want to point out how bad it is and kindly ask people to stop paying for the cruelty and abuse and go somewhere else; somewhere more ethical. This is why we included the chapter to point out the difference between charity and activism. Our goals might be the same, but our actions and effectiveness will differ.

We don't just have to do this in tourist hot spots around the world. We can do it in our own home town or city. I've seen people outside coffee shops in Cornwall with banners about the cruelty of the milk industry, mostly in groups but even individuals on their own. This is all it takes. One person with a passion and a message to share and the motivation to stand up and do it. While this is not directly disruptive, it can have a disruptive effect on the businesses that sell the products that are being protested. If someone is outside a butcher shop, then people will be put off going inside. Of course, we have to face the fact that they may go elsewhere to buy their dead flesh, but perhaps they won't. If they stop and engage with the protester, then there is the opportunity to have another conversation that could lead to new vegans!

One thing that I've noticed vegans doing is going on to Facebook and leaving bad reviews of businesses. I've mixed feelings about this. On the one hand, a restaurant serving faux grois is disgusting, but so is eating the other parts of any animal; so should we leave reviews for them all? Perhaps we should! If we have been to a restaurant and had a bad experience or their vegan dish is awful or the service not good, then we should leave a review that we feel they deserve. But we have to think about why we would single one business out for one animal product when they are all bad. We also have to evaluate if this behaviour is productive and will it make a difference?

However, there are occasions where this could and perhaps should be used as a last resort. I saw a campaign against an animal sanctuary who was preparing to hold a no fire night with fireworks. In an animal sanctuary! How irresponsible and a completely ridiculous thing for an animal sanctuary to be doing. The campaigners messaged the sanctuary asking them politely to stop, contacted them numerous times, but they refused to cancel the event. So what was left to do? The campaigners threatened to go to the papers and the press and even threatened to hold a protest on the night of the event. Still, no shift and the sanctuary was holding their ground. All that was left to do to counter this irresponsible behaviour and animal abuse was to leave comments on their Facebook page and encourage others to do so too. As well as comments, negative reviews would put pressure on the sanctuary to put the animals first and not put them through the stress of fireworks so close to where they lived and slept.

Other places like Zoos, Circuses, and Seaworld's are obvious places that we should all be leaving bad reviews. They torture the animals and treat these amazing social, intelligent creatures in the most appalling ways possible. In fact, Seaworld Orlando has removed the review option from their Facebook pages so no reviews can be left. But there are still websites like trip advisor where it's possible and also on Google business pages where the reviews show up on the search.

Another way to disrupt that has a more positive angle is to go to where people are visiting and promote another attraction that has no animal abuse or exploitation or even any animals at all. If people go to one location but have the opportunity to visit different attractions, there is a high chance they won't have time to do both. If you can convince them why they should do one over the other, then you have made a huge achievement.

With social media, we do have the opportunity to reach many people directly. If we have the resources and funds, then we can get messages to people directly through Facebook using content delivered as a targeted advertisement. Dare I say we could even create rumours but this isn't my scene or way to do things, and the truth is bad enough that we really don't have to. With so much abuse and cruelty in the world, we just don't need to make things up, it's hell for the animals as it is.

CHAPTER 15

VOLUNTEERING

"Only a life lived for others is worth living."

- Albert Einstein

Volunteering seems like a great way to help animals and use the experience to encourage others to do so. We designed our Epic Animal Quest around the idea of volunteering with animal charities and organisations. I will say that we have had a mixed experience after our first two years and I think we spent too much time doing it and not enough time doing more effective activism. We have since changed our approach and are now focussing our efforts and attention on other methods of activism. Of course, if we meet an organisation or charity that resonates with us and after due diligence, we find they are worth supporting, we will give our time to them. But overall, our opinion on charities is not super favorable overall, and I know it sounds controversial, but we have learned from a few mistakes and decided that this way isn't the best way for us to make a difference personally and charities are certainly not the most effective way to make a difference and solve problems. After our first two years of being involved with small and large international charities in the UK and abroad, we wrote the Beehive book to put forward a better and more effective way to solve social problems. What we experienced was disheartening, to say the least, but we did see the power of social enterprise, community action, and collaboration and these are areas we are committing a lot of time to now.

We want to make sure that any money we help raise gets spent on the actual cause and animals rather than on expenses, beaurocracy, inefficient and inexperienced management, and high operating costs. With smaller charities, we have found that the money can often be wasted and the level of business experience of the people starting and running the charity has a lot to do with the efficiency and effectiveness of it.

While we have a somewhat cynical view of charities now, we can't forget that some really do help animals and some of them are exceptional. We just made the naive mistake of thinking that every charity had to be started for the right reasons and that everyone in them had to have high ethics. We soon learned that this wasn't the case and although we were disappointed, we took the experience and it has helped shape what we do today. We still work with charities, but we do research and ask a series of specific questions before we give any time or money to them.

So how to decide who to volunteer with and if your volunteering is effective and actually helps an animal or helps solve a problem? There are a few things you can do. First, ask lots of questions and don't be afraid to or think that you are being rude. A charity or nonprofit should publish their accounts to the public and should be accountable for every penny they raise and spend. So ask how much they raise, how much they spend on operational costs before they spend on the actual problem. Clarify what the problem is that they are trying to solve and ask them how successful they have been.

You will no doubt find that most charities or organisations will never have enough funding or enough money to do what they want to. However, if you hear that 'when we get another £1000 we will be able to do x,y,z,' then you must question why they have to wait and if you find, like we did all too often, that once they get that £1000 they suddenly need another £1000, take heed and treat that as a warning sign. Often problems don't need a lot of money to solve, and if an organisation is continually chasing money and not solving any of the problems, you have to question their effectiveness.

If you volunteer with an organisation, ask them how your time will help. Tell them about the skills do you have, what you think you can do to help the most. I made the mistake of thinking that I would help by feeding and cleaning the animals and their enclosures, but I didn't consider just how valuable writing, filming, photography, marketing, and web design would be to a charity. These are skills they often lack or certainly lack time to carry them out effectively themselves. So if you have skills in specific areas, make sure you let them know and take the time to find out what they really need and see if you have it already to give them. Your skills could be worth far more than you think.

Charities are businesses too, there really aren't that many differences. So you will find that people are just the same as those who you would encounter in any business. A manager or owner/founder is not always going to appreciate you making suggestions or being critical of what they are doing. If you can provide a solution to something they need, ego and pride can prevent them from accepting it. This is very strange, but the structure of organisations who operate as a pyramid place the founder at the top, and this can often cause the misbelief that they have to have all the answers. We wrote a lot about this in Beehive. Some will, of course, welcome feedback and really appreciate your skills, so if you find people who behave like that, there is a good chance that they are the best ones to work with.

Gratitude is not something that everyone gives out. We found that many people expect help for free and do not appreciate it at all. At the other end of the scale, we have met people who are immensely grateful for the smallest of tasks that you do for them. There is nothing worse than finishing your regular job and then volunteering in your spare time, only to hear the founder/manager commenting that they have been working too many hours themselves and not acknowledging that you are actually working more hours than them in total! I know this sounds like such a stupid and small concern, but believe, me, time is valuable, and when it's not appreciated it does make us question what we are doing and why we are doing it when it's not appreciated. This lack of gratitude will no doubt seep through to donors, paid employees, and other areas of the charity which will, in time, make it ineffective if it isn't already. We could easily direct our time to other causes and have a more significant impact.

Volunteering makes you feel great, but I have to question whether it benefits the person volunteering more than it helps the animals. There is nothing wrong with doing something that makes us feel good, but we have to be honest with ourselves. This whole chapter sounds like volunteering is a terrible idea and in many cases, it can be. It's not the most effective form of activism, but it is activism none the less, and in the right places it can really help the animals.

We volunteered to feed animals, and it wasn't a great experience, but then we volunteered in a different place and found that socialising the animals was very important. Involving the children in volunteering was something we felt was important to teach them about compassion and helping for the sake of helping. In the UK, we found that the insurance wouldn't allow under 18 years old to volunteer but in Cambodia, this wasn't an issue at all. Still, we found that some places welcomed the children and were really happy to have them around, but then others allowed them to come but the vibe wasn't great, and the experience wasn't either.

We quickly learned that cleaning and feeding wasn't the best use of our time and ended up working on creating content and using our marketing experience to help raise money. In one case, we raised and donated around $5000 which was a considerable amount of money. We found that that money got swept into a bigger pot of money and not spent on actually changing anything or solving any problems. It crossed our minds that we could have raised a fraction of that money and then put it to directly solve a problem we encountered. So we could volunteer and end up inevitably raising money for a charity steeped in bureaucracy, or we could raise money and put that money to a direct use. Working with other vegan activists who are clearly not acting out of payment or financial reward, means that fundraising and bidding for funding is rarely, if ever, a conversation.

In some cases, charities rely solely on volunteers to get the jobs done. We were part of a Pagoda Patrol on Phnom Penh where we went around and brought cats and dogs back to a centre to be desexed and vaccinated. Without volunteers, the program was ineffective, and without volunteers, nothing would have happened. Even though this was the case, there seemed to be a divide between the people who were paid people who volunteered and we were once accused of putting work on the paid employees when we tried to get more animals desexed. It was a strange experience, and this was one charity where the volunteering experience was not effective for the cause or fun for us, and we certainly weren't appreciated. In fact, none of the volunteers received many thanks, and there was much complaining about them behind their back. We have since learned that this volunteering program at the Pagodas has failed but it took two years to fail and cost a lot of money. Many of us told the charity that it wasn't working and that the model was flawed for many reasons, but we were all ignored. Eventually, the program failed because no one would volunteer under the circumstances we talk about here, but how much money was wasted by the founder through marketing, meetings, expenses, talks at international Expos and all the other areas that they spent time on to raise money for it?

So seek out places to volunteer with caution and consider whether your time could be spent better elsewhere. When we made the switch to focus more on activism than volunteering, we made much more progress and had a much bigger impact. During our time in Cambodia, we gathered footage about the dog meat trade and also from undercover at various pig, cow, and duck slaughterhouses. Charities wanted the dog meat footage, especially even though they didn't have any idea how they would use it other than raising awareness and raising money in the UK and other countries outside of where the footage was taken. We argued that raising aware- ness and money in the UK didn't help the dogs or people in Cambodia and we just felt uncomfortable throughout the whole experience. The idea they had was to spend a year developing a strategy and then use the footage to implement it. They even suggested using the footage to funnel money into another project run by the charity we had volunteered with that had nothing to do with the dog meat trade and was already heavily funded yet unproductive and inefficient. This same charity had also explicitly told us that they would not comment on the dog meat trade in case their NGO status was revoked and that we should not mention them when talking or writing about the dog meat trade. It all left a bad taste in our mouths.

The idea of giving footage to someone who needs a year to develop a strategy on how best to use it just didn't fit with our goals. To contrast this, we managed to get undercover foot- age from a specific slaughterhouse and sent that to PETA. They had a use for it immediately, and the use was clear and directed towards the country of origin. Raising money or awareness was was not a discussion but we felt that any funds raised from it would be used to promote Veganism, so if they benefitted from it, it would be a good thing. Raising aware- ness about eating dogs doesn't stop the dogs from being eaten and taking a year or so to 'develop a strategy' didn't sound like a good plan to us. PETA just used the footage and got on with it right away. The only strategy that made sense to them and us was to get the footage in front of as many people as possible and make sure those people were the ones who ate pigs and would need to see it the most. Incidentally, the other charity was not interested in Pigs as they focussed on domestic animals.

So volunteer with caution and make sure you are able to use your unique skills to have the biggest impact possible. Look at collaboration and community action as an alternative to volunteering, and seek out groups who are already working together in your area. If you can help them, then you may find you can be more productive than just by volunteering for a charity. Social enterprises can be amazing if you can find them, and if you can work with them, you will see a completely different approach that is sustainable and scalable.

CHAPTER 16

SOCIAL MEDIA

"Don't say anything online that you wouldn't want plastered on a billboard with your face on it."

- Erin Bury

Posting and joining in conversations on social media is a great way to start talking about Veganism and getting into Vegan activism. If you have a smartphone, tablet or laptop, then you can open an account with Facebook, YouTube (you don't have to post videos to join conversations), Twitter, Medium, Pinterest, Instagram, Snapchat, and the many other platforms available. This is something pretty much anyone can do. If you don't like getting into 'conversations' in the comment sections (and let's face it, these are often awful places to spend time) then just don't! Post memes, pictures, videos, your own thoughts, put it out there and let people see it. If someone insults you or makes a comment that makes you feel uncomfortable, either ignore it, reply to it, or delete it. You don't have to be dragged into their negative world, and you should never feel obliged to be. Some people like arguing or even 'trolling' other pages and posts and a good debate can be fun. Most of the time, though, the conversations like this just end up being insulting and argumentative, and nothing is achieved. I ignore the idiot comments but engage in the ones that offer civil debate, and these are the conversations that can help us make progress.

Another way to approach your Social Media Activism is to take a positive approach. Post things that show why Veganism is so amazing for the animals, our health, and our environment. Show the good side to being vegan and lead by your own example. You can even spend time helping new vegans with questions they have and supporting others when they need it. Share recipes, promote Vegan alternative products and share the links, and promote companies who supply Vegan clothes, cleaning products, food, entertainment and anything else that is cruelty-free.

I like to use social media to share our book, projects, blog posts, videos, Vlogs, podcast, thoughts, and photographs. With our Epic Animal Quest, we cover all the major social media, Instagram, Twitter, Facebook, Medium, Anchor, and Youtube, and use our own website as a home base. We share our lifestyle and write about our animal rights activities all around the world. I write about all sorts of topics from Vegan travel and family to Vegan arguments and activism. We make videos about animal rights issues and Veganism and document our positive Vegan travel family lifestyle in a daily vlog. At the time of writing, I really favour Facebook and am focussing on that more than the other platforms. We still post on the others, but for us, conversations are better had on Facebook and we really enjoy the interaction the platform allows.

Social Media has an outlet for everyone, no matter how confident or talented you are. Everyone has a talent or passion, and you can use that to promote Veganism and dominate a niche on social media. If you like taking photographs, then you have Instagram and Facebook. If cartoons are your thing, then use Tumblr too. Some people - and I really struggle with this but growing more comfortable - like being in front of the camera, and so YouTube comes easy to them. You can also use YouTube to show off slideshows, animations, and presentations, so you don't have to be in front of the camera yourself. As a writer, I like to write above all else, so sharing our blog posts on all the platforms works for me. I can link to specific posts I have written to answer peoples questions, and I can promote my books (and other peoples books) that have been written to help Vegans. Quotes work well on Twitter to get people commenting, and memes on Facebook make excellent conversation starters.

It is a long game we are playing here, and sadly we can't make change happen overnight. It may be that it's our children that see the real change, so we have to lay the foundations for them. If we are to keep playing the game of change for many years, then we have to keep ourselves mentally (and physically) healthy. I plan to do this by keeping my sense of humour and developing a mix of mediums by which to share my experiences, information, and thoughts. Show the terrible, horrific side of the animal agriculture industry but balance it with the many positives of a Vegan lifestyle. We often say that we are living the dream in a world full of nightmares, and Facebook definitely shows us that.

Social Media allows a drip feeding effect that will slowly build up and up over time. If more people add their owns 'drips' of insight and information, then the bowl of Veganism will fill much quicker. If we don't increase the input from other Vegans, then the process of change will be slow, and that is why I feel it is so important for every Vegan to get involved in more ways than just their diet choice. We all have to get active in activism.

Although I love writing and social media, one thing that I think is super important is that we get away from the computer from time to time and take part in a 'real life' physical protest or meet up. Not only will it give you more fuel to use when you are lighting your Vegan fires across the internet, but it will give you the chance to talk to real people and have real conversations, and even make great friends! I find this is much more effective and the conversations mostly remain civil, friendly, and informative. Talking to people face to face is my favourite way to communicate what Veganism is and why we are Vegan. Seeing peoples physical reactions is a good way to gauge effectiveness and can often tell us much more than what they say.

One thing we quickly learned was to avoid engaging with internet trolls, and we covered this in the chapter devoted to it earlier. Trolls exist off the screen in real life too, and if we come across people who are just trying to get a rise, we generally try and avoid conversations with them.

People have to be ready to make a change, and they have to be open to new information and ideas. Whenever someone posts a picture of a steak or a bacon sandwich on a Vegan social media feed, you know they are not there to learn something new or engage in a rational conversation or even a debate. They are there for their own entertainment; nothing else. So we choose to avoid these trolls and tend not to engage. If someone chooses to join in on one of your own posts with a steak or bacon picture, then it's easy to delete the comment and block or ban them if they keep bugging you. Or you could leave it on there and let others chip in and comment.

Once you decide on how you will use social media and what platforms you prefer, you can randomly post when you have the time, or you can get tactical. If you have created content and want to share it with many people outside your circle of friends, then Facebook is a platform that stands out as a quick way to get something set up so you can take your online social media activism to the next level. Once you have a personal Facebook account, you can quickly create a page. The page can be a cause, so you don't have to be registered as a business or anything like that, and you can add any pictures you like just like on a personal page. Posting is pretty much the same, but you have the option of boosting a post to more people or creating Facebook ads. Both methods come at a cost but allow you to focus on a very niche and targeted audience. If you have created a piece of content about fur used on jackets for example, then you can target people who like the pages of the businesses who sell the jackets. Your post will pop up on their timeline and might get them thinking. Paying for boosting and advertising like this is something that has to be strategic, and some research would really help maximise your efforts and money if you choose to do it. The great thing about Facebook is the ability to target such niche audiences but also to analyse the results of the boost or ad. There is so much information that can be taken from it and you can use that information to assess if it worked, what you might do better, and whether or not it should be repeated. We have books on marketing, specifically for social enterprises and non-profits in the animal rights world, so if this is of interest to you, check them out on our website.

Most of us have experience of using social media for our own personal lives, the cost of entry is zero money and little time to learn how to use it. You may find that once you start sharing Vegan posts, your friends and family won't engage much and they may even stop following you. This is to be expected, but don't let it put you off. If anything, it is a good filter of who really is your friend and who is supportive of your compassionate lifestyle choice.

We recently saw that you can also volunteer as a mentor with a few Vegan Facebook pages and help other new Vegans to Go Vegan and Stay Vegan! Just by commenting, replying to questions, giving advice, and pointing people in the right direction can really help people to stay Vegan and save many animals in the process.

So give it a go and see what happens! Most importantly, remember it's social media, so be social, have fun, share, share, share, and engage with other people and their content too!

CHAPTER 17

LETTER WRITING & LOBBYING

"The corporations don't have to lobby the government anymore. They are the government."

- Jim Hightower

Letter writing and petitions are something I am guilty of spending little time on, but they can be very effective in changing policies, especially where companies and their PR departments are concerned. Some can be a bit dubious like one I encountered recently asking for people to add their email to a petition to stop Japan killing street cats in one location. People were told that if they could get enough to 'sign', then the cats would be saved. The petition in the UK had no chance of being effective, the cats were always going to be killed, and the charity could blame the lack of signatures for them not being able to stop it happening. They then had thousands of emails to send out fundraising requests to. So while petitions can be effective, be careful which ones you spend time on.

I find that businesses are the best ones to focus on. Airlines that fly animals like Macaque monkeys from Asia to the west for medical research have been boycotted, and many have chosen to stop participating in this transport. If you know of an airline, like Air France (at time of writing) that still participates, then an email, a Facebook message, or a letter can be effective ways to get their attention and let them know how many of us feel this is totally unacceptable and we will not ever use them. If a petition can be started that gathers many names and email addresses, the effect can, and real change can happen in response to it.

Travel companies who advertise Seaworld and other animal prisons as part of their entertainment packages will change their ways if enough of us contact them and make public our views. We have been gifted this amazing thing that is social media that allows us to get the truth in front of millions of people who otherwise would never have seen it. Some say that the internet is changing us, but I say that what it is really doing is exposing us for who we really are and amplifying it for the world to see. So let's take this tool and use it to point out that animals kept in captivity for entertainment are cruel and unnecessary. It doesn't have to be all negative, we can live by the Vegan definition and promote the alternative. Take Phuket, there is a dolphin centre that offers the public three dolphin display every day. They say they are set up to protect these endangered species, yet they are linked to be complicit in the horrors of the dolphin capture and executions that go on it Tajin (you can learn so much about this from the documentary called The Cove). When we visited places like this, our goal could be to use a number of these activism methods to disrupt the centre and affect them where it hurts; in their profits. While we do things to disrupt, we can also promote local boat trips that take visitors out into the ocean to see the dolphins living their lives in their natural environment free from hoops of fire and humans riding or being dragged along on their backs.

While a petition or letter probably won't work on the dolphin centre itself, it will work on hotels, tour guides, airlines, and holiday companies who might include it in their itineraries. If we can write to them explaining why the centre is bad for the dolphins and provide better alternatives at the same time, then we have an opportunity to make a difference for the animals and prevent further animals being bred in captivity or plucked from their families in the wild. If enough people sign the petition and the story is compelling, then you could present everything you have done to a newspaper and hope they will take the story.

Social media is also a tool we can use to show companies there are thousands, perhaps even millions of people who are not happy with what they are doing to the animals, our health, and our planet that we all have to share. We can encourage others to message the Facebook pages of organisations like the dolphin centre.

Be aware of some fake petition sites too, as they are set up just to get email addresses and are not even used as real petitions or presented to anyone. Facebook can be full of these, so maybe do a quick search online to see if they are legit. Most of these bad guys have a name for themselves, and people will have written about it online, so it should come up with a quick google search. Of course, the petitions issued by organisations like PETA, Viva, and The Vegan Society are at first glance the ones to trust, but even so, find out where the source is and make sure it is the organisation issuing the petition and not some scam artist. These large organisations and their petitions are sometimes the only way to get through to make changes on a governmental level, so they are worth taking part in for sure.

Lobbying is another area you can get involved with when letter writing. If there is an issue that can be changed on a governmental level, then writing to your local member of parliament (MP) or representative is the thing to do in the first instance. If you can get other people to join you in this action, then you can make an appointment and take the dis-

cussion further. We have written to MP's as part of campaigns before and found that they do write back. Often, they
have their reasons why it won't go further or at least the reas-
surance that this is an important issue and the usual bumf
that comes from these windbags. But, this is our process if we
want to go down this avenue.

Letter writing is something we can all pretty much do,
and as long as we have a smartphone, tablet or computer, we
can take letter writing to the next level. Once a letter is written, we can reuse it for similar campaigns and even publish it
online for others to download and copy to save time. We can
email it to as many places as we want and it's free to do. So if
you feel like this is something you can get involved with, go
for it! Sites like PETA and Viva - while each has their own
negatives - are excellent sources to bring causes to light and
lay out the case as to why petitioning and letter writing will
help combat them and their related issues.

CHAPTER 18

GET A JOB OR BUILD A CAREER

"When you find a job you love, you'll never work again."

- Winston Churchill

Working for a non-profit or social enterprise can be a great way to earn a living while being part of something that is making a difference for the animals. If you can get a job for somewhere like The Vegan Society or Viva, then you can really be involved in an organisation that is leading the way in the world of Veganism and showing people how to go Vegan, stay Vegan, and get involved in activism. Even simple things like providing free flyers to activists is something that Viva are doing that is getting the right messages and the truth out there and into the face of people who need to see and are grateful for it. Also, Veganuary is becoming very effective and reaching many people around the world.

Try not to make the mistake we made in Cambodia, and believe that all animal charities and people running them are making a difference or solving a problem. I go into detail about this in the section on volunteering, so I don't want to repeat it for you here. Some animal charities are, of course, doing amazing things for the animals, but there are also many who are winning huge amounts of funding, donations, and sponsorships but not solving anything. How many times have you seen a charity grow but while the problem they set up to solve doesn't shrink? Often, the charity will find more problems to get involved with just to win funding and then this takes them away from the focus and the reasons why they started the charity in the first place. I know this is quite a cynical view of charities, but Rachael and I have worked for a number of charities for many years and we have seen the inner workings and even been part of them.

We are a social enterprise and try to find charities and organisations who are doing amazing effective work and collaborate with them. If we can help them, then we can help the animals through them. We will happily work for less money if we know that they are doing something to make a difference and are living up to their mission statement that we also believe in. Unfortunately, we do have to earn money to live, but if we can earn that money and work for a good cause, we can feel much better about the money we earn. I know that I do a better job for an organisation that is helping animals - including the human animals - and sometimes when I work for free, I am much more invested in the problem and work much harder. We are not motivated by money so as long as we earn enough to do what we want to do, we are happy. Our goal with Epic Animal Quest is to sell enough of our books so we can always work for free within projects, collaborations, and organisations we are passionate about and then use excess profits to pay for whatever is needed. We will be in control of where and how the money is spent so we know it is all spent on the animals and not on expenses, excess wages, and things that are a waste of money and don't contribute to solving the problem.

One thing we have learned is that it is not a good idea to help charities that are failing or those that are ineffective. An example of this is when we worked with one charity we needed $100 to help one cat per month. Then we worked with another who needed just $20 to help one cat per month. We could help 5 times as many cats by working with the efficient charity. This is now touching on effective altruism, which is a fascinating idea and a growing movement. It is based on the idea that we should use our money, time, and our careers to help the most effective charities. Look out for a book on this coming soon!

Collaboration is something we are passionate about now. Being part of a team of hardworking people who love what they do and are passionate about helping the animals is something that is a joy to be a part of. When like-minded genuine people come together, incredible things can be achieved. We need money to get many things done, but passion, time, and handwork should never be underestimated, and these things can often achieve much more than money alone. Working for an organisation to help the animals and fellow Vegans like The Vegan Society or Viva doesn't mean you have to have a job as a fundraiser. You could get a job in any department just like any organisation with an administrative structure, so there should be a position for everyone. If you like working in call centres, distribution, human resources, or management, all these areas will be available if you are the right fit for the organisation. All of these areas are crucial for them to run efficiently and effectively and there are many job titles available and many organisations like them if you look around.

Most websites have a recruitment page, and even if they aren't advertising any positions, it is well worth getting in touch and registering your interest and sending them a CV. You may even find they can recommend you on to a partner organisation who might be interested in what you have to offer. So put yourself out there, make yourself known and heard, and I hope you get to work for an organisation you believe in and have an awesome time making your living and a career in compassion!

CHAPTER 19

ART

"Artists are here to disturb the peace."

- James Baldwin

Art comes in many forms, and none of us can pin it down to one simple definition. Whether it's visual like graffiti, sculpture, videos, comic books, photography, and realistic paintings, or poems, music, novels, and the spoken word, any art form can be used to get a message across or tell a story. If you are artistic or have a skill in a specific area, then why not use that skill to help the animals?

I like to experiment with lots of different art forms, and it's been interesting to see what works and what doesn't work. When I try something new, I like to set challenges such as a thirty-day comic strip challenge where I created Alfie, a cynical Vegan dog, and put together a newspaper-style comic strip each day for thirty days. I chose topics that were common in Veganism and tried my best to put a light-hearted and comedic twist on it. You can see the results of this challenge here www.epicanimalquest.com/alfie

Another challenge was the one hundred day video challenge where, you guessed it, I made a video each day for one hundred days. During this time, I created different styles of videos including vlogs, podcasts, informative presentations, and short stories, and the experience taught me a lot. I found what I liked to do and ended up creating more and more videos after the challenge all about our daily lives as a Vegan travel family and also about animals we met on our travels. This also got me into taking photographs, and I discovered how awesome the medium was. From this experience, we built services into our social enterprise that allowed us to trade videos for accommodation, food, and entertainment as well as helping other organisations to promote their work and raise money. This wasn't something we ever planned when we started our Epic Animal Quest, so it goes to show you can learn a new skill, practice and get good at it, then implement it in your life and even grow a career out of it!

An activist friend of ours runs her own art business called www.hepzibahpink.com where she creates awesome drawings and paintings in print and originals and also hand-stamped jewellery and cutlery. Much of her work is around animal rights and Veganism, and she has been able to build a business around two things she is passionate about art and Veganism. Just like writing books, if you are good at something and can make a living doing it, why not try and see how you can use that skill and make your subject Veganism? If we can earn money doing something we love and help the animals at the same time, then everyone wins. Rather than spend forty to eighty hours a week working for someone else's dreams, why not take a step out of the norm and break away from the rat race to work on your own?

You don't have to use art as a way to make a living (I can't help see opportunities to create income) to have a positive effect on animal rights and Vegan activism. If art is a hobby for you then again, use it to help the animals in whatever way you can. If you can draw, then chalking is a perfect activity to get into and you can spend a few hours creating a mural in a park or on the streets, but be ready to wash it away if you have to. You can read more on this in the chapter devoted to chalking in this book.

If you have an experience that touches you when you are out and about or taking part in activism, then write or draw about it or express it in any way you can. Different people will react and connect to different art forms, so use what you have to put across your feelings and emotions, and hopefully, you will connect with someone on some level. Share your experiences and paint the picture with words or paints, and never be embarrassed or afraid to share your work with the world. I remember when I first wrote some poems. I was nervous about sharing them on Facebook, and still am, to be honest, but I am glad I did. Even if only one person reads them, then they have a chance of igniting an emotion in their mind, and that spark could grow into something much greater. Of course, poems are not for everyone, but anything you can create has to be shared. Once it is out into the world, so is your intention, and this intention is a very important part of making the change. You are announcing to the world how you feel and stating clearly that you won't take part in the cruelty and exploitation of animals and are fighting to help them.

Seeing a simple cartoon or an elaborate painting that is focussed on Veganism and animal rights is something that can really grab people's attention. In a flood of Facebook posts about peoples evening meals and gym selfies, a unique and original piece of art will always stand out and get noticed. If it strikes a cord, then it gets shared and has the potential to reach thousands, even millions of people. Of course, this is rare, but the opportunity is still there. After all, everyone has the same upload and post buttons!

So get creative and think about how you can use your skills to create masterpieces that will make people think and tell a story. We all have a gift in us, a certain thing that we are good at, so search for it and then use it to change the world!

CHAPTER 20

LEARNING

"Learn to be thankful for what you already have, while you pursue all that you want."

- Jim Rohn

This is a huge one for me. Learning what to say when people come at you with a barrage of objections and arguments against Veganism is perhaps the most important things we can do as Vegan activists. I wrote The Vegan Argument; why there really is an answer for everything, because I felt I had to have the answers at hand for whenever anyone confronted me or took an interest. I viewed it as my obligation to know what I was talking about and to give sound and reasonable answers so that I argued the case correctly. The Vegan Argument is solid, and there is no acceptable moral argument for eating animals who we do not need to eat. Once we can answer every objection rationally and logically - and there are around one hundred standard ones that we covered in the book - we can show that there really is an answer for every objection. When those answers are given, there is no direction to go in other than the Vegan one. Not everyone takes that road - even when they have all the answers and know about all the cruelty - but if we can get them to the fork in the road where they have to make decision to carry on being complicit in the cruelty, murder, and exploitation or choose compassion and live a Vegan lifestyle, then that is an awesome thing for us to do. If we can help them to take the right road by offering support and a constant drip feeding of information, then even better.

When we choose the red pill and realise the world we grew up in is contracted of lies and facades, we can't help but take in the new information and the new facts that were hidden from us for so long. All we have to do is learn the new information so that we can inform others and answer the questions when they come up.

I will always remember the first encounter that we had just two days into our new Vegan life. A neighbour who was a retired healthcare professional told us that our children could be taken away from us because they were vegan! She informed us of one single case where a family had their children taken into care because they were 'malnourished on a

Vegan diet.' They were working parents, middle class, (as if that made a difference) and they were very intelligent people, according to her. She raised the protein argument amongst others and was adamant that this was a bad idea and that we needed to research it.

Before we made the decision to go vegan, we had many concerns of our own and spent weeks researching everything we could find. The book we wrote some six months later was a result of our research. This lady had no idea that we had thoroughly looked into our new vegan diet and had taken all measures to ensure our children would be healthy and happy. She also neglected to talk about the thousands of children who weren't vegan, but who were also taken into care because of malnutrition. This is the problem that we find over and over again. One case will be reported by the media of one vegan person in a decade, but the thousands of non-vegan stories are not mentioned. If they were, the newspapers would be reporting on meat eaters being taken into care daily. But when a vegan hits the headlines, it's suddenly newsworthy.

This kind of mild hysteria is not limited to old retired and misinformed ex-health professionals in Cornish villages. That same year, there were reports that the Italian government were trying to make it against the law to feed children a vegan diet! It seems ignorance knows no bounds. As parents who only want the best for our children, this question is probably the one that could potentially cause the most of-fence, especially when you get it for the first time. When the lady told us we could lose our children, we were really offen-ded and annoyed, to say the least, but we soon realised this would be a normal interaction and that we had to prepare for it and get used to it. So how can we handle objections like these without getting emotional, and should we even have to deal with people like this?

I think we have to respond to this just as we do all the other objections. It will be much easier when we know all the answers and are prepared to give them in a cool and calcu-lated manner. One main objection that you are going to hear for many years to come, from many people you know and meet, is the old 'where will you get your protein?' I'll use this question and answer it to show that when you know the an-swer, it is easily handled. You could thank the person for their concern and then ask them the following questions:

How much protein should we eat each day?
Where can we get protein from?
What is protein?
What does protein do?

The chances are that if the person knows the answers to these questions, they wouldn't be asking the questions in the first place! When they reveal they have no idea how much protein we all need, you can help them by letting them know the answer. Here is a concise answer that covers pretty much the whole argument that you might like to put into your own words or just copy:

"I used to ask that question too. But then I researched exactly what protein is, how much I need, and where I can get it. We only need 0.6-0.8 grams of protein per kilo of body weight per day. I can easily get all this from fruits, nuts, and vegetables, as long as I eat 2000-2500 calories. Eating a varied diet makes sure I get all the essential amino acids that my body needs to make all the different proteins. The best part is that my protein comes without saturated fats and cholesterol, and is packed with fibre to help me digest and break down my food. Protein really isn't an issue for vegans."

If they have other objections, you can answer in the same way and ask them questions you pretty much know they won't have the answers to. Highlighting their ignorance in a nice friendly way will allow you to keep the conversation going and give you the opportunity to drop a few more truth bombs on them. Once you get the chance to have a conversation, you could go on, 'in fact, do you know that eating meat is actually bad for you? The World Health Organisation has found through hundreds of studies, that eating bacon, red meat, and processed meats actually cause cancer?' Or, 'Do you know that the 10 biggest causes of death in this country are all linked to eating a standard western diet that includes meat?' Or, 'Did you know that Vegans reportedly live, on average, 10 years longer than meat eaters?'

Any objections misinformed and opinionated people give you, can be handled easily when you have the knowledge at hand. It's easier said than done, though but ignore the mindless statements and instead focus on the objection they are giving you. Then use the opportunity to highlight their ignorance, give them the correct information, and drop in some reasons why going vegan is the best option not just for your children, but for the entire planet.

CHAPTER 21

WRITE A BOOK

"If you want to be a writer, you must do two things above all others: read a lot and write a lot."

- Stephen King

You've probably heard it said that everyone has a book in them? Even though Christopher Hitchens added to the phrase "perhaps that's where it should say", if you love writing and have something to say, then writing a book is a brilliant life goal to achieve and one that can be combined to help the animals.

Writing a book can be an amazing way to get your point of view out into the world and appeal to people in a unique way. We all have something to say, and if we can articulate it into the written word, then a book can be a powerful tool to help the Vegan movement. Whether you choose to write about food, ethics, environment, health or lifestyle, a book that appeals to a niche audience can really change minds. Imagine you write a book, and because of your book, one hundred people Go Vegan? Of those one hundred people, if half stay Vegan for life and go on to encourage other people to do it too, then your book will have an exponential effect and will be the seed that sprouts into thousands of compassionate minds!

The thought of writing a book can be overwhelming, how many pages, what should the cover look like, where and how do I publish it, and how long will it take? Many questions like these will come up and need to be addressed, but it's an exciting process and experience that I am sure you will love and hate! Writing the first draft is probably the easiest bit as you can just blurt out all your thoughts and get them all on the screen or on the paper. Once the first draft is complete, then it's time for the first edit. Some people do the whole draft then edit it. After writing my first book, The Vegan Argument, and then writing a blog for years, I sometimes prefer to write a chapter, then edit it and get it finished and ready to go, then move onto the next one. Breaking it down like this into smaller tasks makes the whole endeavour much more manageable, and for me, I find I work faster and with better end results. This wouldn't work so well on a fictional piece as the plot needs to develop as each chapter is written, and the edit would work better covering all the chapters at once.

When all the chapters are done, I go over the book again and make sure as best I can that everything is in order. You can use an editor, of course, and this comes with a cost, or you can choose to self-edit. If you can afford it, it's almost always going to be better to pay an editor. Publishing is a separate issue, and we publish our books ourselves with Kindle. The great thing about this is that you can post revisions and new editions really easily and at no extra cost. The addition of CreateSpace and Kindle Paperback means we can even sell printed books that are printed to order and all this is taken care of by Amazon. You have to spend a bit of time getting the formatting right but having the printed copies available means you sell many more books. Readers can also take the ISBN that Kindle gives you for free, and order your book from popular bookstores. We find we sell roughly two times as many printed books than Kindle downloads. Kindle offers some marketing tools like the KDP program and paid advertising. If you have a book that is perhaps shorter or that you don't want to charge for, then KDP is something you should look into as it gives you the potential to 'sell' more books for free.

How many pages you write really depends on what and how much you have to say. On average, a published non-fiction book that you would see in print and in bookstores would be between forty and ninety thousand words. Kindle ebooks can be a lot less, and some even have just ten thousand words, and even fewer, but forty is a good target to aim for. I have found that a one to two thousand word count per chapter is a good amount to get a point across or explore an idea. It makes for a good reading duration for the reader, and in the type of non-fiction I like to write, my books are written with the idea that people can delve into any chapter at any time (after the introduction) and that they will stand alone from the book while being part of the whole. If people choose to read right through continuously, then the books will still work, but each chapter will be clearly defined. When you take this one to two thousand word count as a guide, you can see that thirty to forty chapters (including your introduction, prologue, conclusion, and acknowledgements) will make a good sized non-fiction work.

Once you know that you want to write thirty or forty chapters, then you can lay them out and get busy writing each one. If you can do the first draft of a chapter in one day, then edit the chapter in one other day, it would take a couple of months to get a book written. Then with a final edit and polish, plus all the formatting and cover designs, you could push yourself to get a book written in three months. Everyone will write at different speeds, and some books need more research than others, but if you can write about your own experiences, you have already done all the research you need. If you work out how long it takes you to write five hundred or a thousand words, then you can calculate how long it will take you. Even five hundred words a day will see your first draft and edit done within eight months, so with the other elements, just five hundred words a day could result in a book within one year! Some people can write books much quicker than this, and just like in any profession, the more you do it, the quicker you can get. Some days I will write ten thousand words, while others maybe two to five thousand. It is not unusual for some authors to write and publish a book a month, and that is what we are aiming for at the moment.

The cover is important, after all, books really are judged by them, so time spent on this is essential. Have a look at the other books in your niche, and see which ones sell the best. See what stands out and think about how you can make yours different. I chose white, blue, and green for The vegan Argument, as no one else was selling a book with those colour combinations in the way I used them. You can design your own cover, or pay someone else to do it. Photos can work well if you have one that tells a story or portrays a powerful message. The font is very important, and you have pretty much unlimited options. I spent hours looking at other books and their covers, seeing why they worked and what I liked about them. Imitation and inspiration are great, but straight up copying is not cool at all and plagiarism is the biggest and most frowned upon crime amongst creatives and writers. Be influenced, inspired, and driven by other influential artists, but don't copy their talent and work; develop your own.

We chose to make writing the major part of our Epic Animal Quest social enterprise and felt that if we were making a living writing, then we could do it writing about the things we are most passionate about. Words live on forever, and something written two thousand years ago can touch people and inspire them to act. We combine words with our pictures and videos on our blog and social media, but the power of the written word alone should never be underestimated.

Listening to music can help with the first step of writing the first draft. Some songs with too many words don't work as they distract, but I find classical, or rock works for me. Recently I discovered Metallica and Iron Maiden made by word count go right up, but you can't beat a bit of Mozart for every stage of the writing process. Rock is not so good for editing in my experience, but I don't think you can beat it when you have a set time to hit a set word count. This is a great tip that I've used when I wanted to get a lot done in a short time. Set a ten-minute timer and then see how many words you can type. Then, have a quick break, and go again and try to beat your score! Repeat this as much as you want, and you will be amazed at how much you can write in even one hour. I learned about this when I joined a local group who were all taking part in Nanowrimo, which is an international initiative to get people writing. Each year during November, people take part to write a novel in one month. The word count is set at fifty thousand, and you only compete with yourself. You share your ongoing word count, though, and it's a great way to keep motivated and know that other people are taking part too. It's a really cool thing to do, and I believe there is another Nanowrimo event around March, but November is the main event.

All you need to write a book, edit, and format it for publication on Kindle and Createspace, is a Word or Pages software. We purchased Scrivener a few years ago, and this made the job of writing and organising our work far better. The way it lays out each section, chapter, notes, and research is amazing and it's very user-friendly. It gives you many options you just don't get with Word or Pages, and for the money, it is definitely worth it. Since I purchased it, I found the whole writing process much more fun and efficient. Thought I mainly write for non-fiction, I have tried my hand at fiction, and the Scrivener tools are perfect for characters, notes, and every other aspect a novelist might need. You can switch easily and quickly between a draft mode and a pinboard mode so you can see plot points, character details, and chapter summaries all on one screen in a very nice layout.

You may think that after all this effort, you just won't sell any books. After all, no one has heard of you, and this might well be your first written work on the chosen subject. I would urge you not to think like this. I read that the average non-fiction book in the US sells around two hundred and fifty books per year and just two thousand in its lifetime. In the first ten months, my book sold over two hundred and fifty and is growing month by month. With this second book and more to follow, these numbers will only grow and grow. Our chosen topic is an evergreen choice and appeals to many people of all ages. Although it's not timeless, Veganism and animal rights will be an issue that we need to promote for many years, even generations. Adding to the literature on the subject can only be a good thing, and the more of us who do it, the better chance we have of making a difference.

Here is my pledge to you. If you write a book about Veganism and animal rights, I will promote it on my website and social media to help you spread the word. Just get in touch, and let me know all the links and details and I would love to help if I can. One awesome thing you can do to support your book is to start a blog. It's free to do on sites like www.wordpress.com, or you can pay a small amount each month and have your own platform and web space. If you can, I would highly recommend having your own domain and web space as you choose who controls and advertises on it. More on this in the chapter 'Start a Blog'. If a Blog doesn't appeal to you, then definitely use your social media platforms to promote your work and post quotes, memes, even videos of you talking about it and share it with as many people as you can.

So give it a go and get that book you always dreamed of writing out into your reality and in front of people who need to read it for a change to happen. Use your talent to help the animals and join the community of writers who are campaigning every day for animal rights around the world. Words are powerful and the right words presented to the right person at the right time can change their world and yours too!

CHAPTER 22

SOCIAL ENTERPRISE

"If you aren't making a difference in other people's lives, you shouldn't be in business - it's that simple."

- Richard Branson

Starting a social enterprise can be a very big commitment, especially if you want to make this your full-time work. But you do have the choice to keep it on a small level and run it alongside your existing job or carrier, and combining this with your activism could be a great move for the animals.

I recommend a social enterprise over a charity for a number of reasons, and we have written about this in depth in our Beehive book. Most importantly, it is because social enterprise tends to be a more sustainable option that means you won't be spending all your time fund-raising and will be able to keep focused on helping the animals. A social enterprise can be set up to solve a problem that helps the animals while bringing in enough money to pay all the costs and leave enough profit left over to fund any activities you feel are important. For our Epic Animal Quest, the social enterprise model works perfectly, and we chose to sell books and other resources because we love to write and feel that our books help people to go Vegan, stay Vegan, and get active in activism. Having a background in business means that we like to sell products and combined with a passion for marketing and social media the books were a great option for us. It will take us a few years to be, and we will continue to work freelance in the meantime, but once established, we will not have to be focused on sales and certainly not fundraising unless for specific causes we get involved with on our travels. Charity can be appealing because you can immediately receive donations for a cause. But the work required to get donations will always continue and as you scale a charity, you will have to scale the fundraising too. With social enterprise, however, your products and customers can scale on their own through smart marketing. So while a charity seems good in the short term, you will always be in the position of chasing donations. Social enterprise will take longer to start up and will cost you personally in investment, but it can last for years, be sustainable, and easier to scale with less effort required.

With our freelance work, we try our best to focus on working with ethical issues, organisations, and social enterprises. Although we have and do work with charities, we have had some bad experiences and so know we have to do our due diligence before jumping in and helping. This is something we have learned our lesson on and strongly encourage anyone interested in working with charities to do too. Ask people in the community what their experience of the charity is. Ask the management team how much they have raised, where the money was spent, what their mission and goals are, and how they monitor the work they are doing. Look at how they treat volunteers, talk about them, and also - a very important one for us - how they treat and talk about their donors. If they seem to lack gratitude but are full of expectation, this could be seen as a bad sign. If you suspect something is not quite right, trust your instinct and leave them to their work. There will be plenty of other opportunities and organisations to help and get involved with.

We also barter our website, marketing, and content creation services working with hotels, restaurants, and businesses to help them develop Vegan menus and make them more Vegan-friendly overall. This helps us to sort accommodation and food, and while we don't earn any money, this service for service exchange saves us a lot! This is also a great way to help make Vegan travel easier for people as we can help provide more dining options as well as cruelty-free shampoos and hygiene products and a focus on eco-friendly practices.

This is an unusual form of activism but one that benefits Vegan travellers and compassionate local businesses as well as the animals!

While in Cambodia, we met an amazing couple who set up a social enterprise called Animal Mama and are working for them freelance producing content and helping to develop their social media. They are a veterinary clinic, pet hospital, and animal wellness centre and their main business is providing top quality veterinary care at prices the local people can afford. They offer the full veterinary care and services you would expect, pet relocation, grooming, boarding, pet products, and other services in areas of pet wellness. With the profits from this enterprise, they help sick, injured, and abandoned street and pagoda animals and pay for all their treatments.

They also work with Wildlife Alliance Cambodia - as Wildlife Alliance Ambassadors - and helped raise money to build enclosures for Macaque monkeys who have been rescued from the cruel tourist trade and an education centre for the protection of elephants. They are also involved in a Gibbon release project with the Wildlife Alliance in the historic Angkor Wat, and we are collaborating with them on a series of videos to highlight the work being carried out by the team. On top of this, have even set up a retirement home for the dogs who can no longer work in the field detecting unexploded ordinance all over the world. Without this Home of

Heroes, the dogs would be euthanised. We worked closely with them for six months during our time in Cambodia and were amazed at what they were doing as a social enterprise and their work far outperformed that of charities who are in the same areas.

While we were there, we came across a pig called Ouk Ouk, who had ben abandoned in a local Pagoda because one of her hooves was black. In Cambodia, it is thought to be unlucky to have anything to do with a pig with a single black hoof. A kind local man who lived at the Pagoda felt that his true Buddhism beliefs were stronger than this superstition, and he chose to show compassion by caring for the pig for the six years she had been there. Sadly, when the pig was four years old, she was hit by a car and was not able to walk. When we came across her, she was six years old and had been immobile for two years. Her hooves were as long as my hand so even if she could have got up, she would not have been able to stand. We put out a call for help, and a couple of local vets offered to cut the hooves but had no tools. Sadly, none of the animal charities was interested in helping as they mainly focused on cats and dogs and their fundraising and marketing were all about just those animals. This is the sad reality of some charities and one reason why we favour social enterprise. We have had the first-hand experience of a charity asking us to purposely photograph dogs (even though we weren't doing anything for them at the time) so their large funder would be happy, and we have also seen things staged to look like more was being done that it really was. While we love social media and marketing and understand that sometimes things are exaggerated, seeing it abused like this just to raise money is sickening.

When we were starting to lose hope and even considered trying to cut the hooves ourselves, Animal Mama located a vet who could do the job properly, and they paid for him to come to Phnom Penh and get the job done. This cost over $500 and the aftercare even more. We continued to visit the Pig and help the gentleman who looked after her. They didn't ask for any donations, and they didn't even care about promoting what they did; they just wanted to help the pig. Having the money available because they earned it through their social enterprise was much more powerful than asking for donations and being strategic about where it is spent. If this were a charity, they would have first run a marketing campaign to raise the money, maybe got some t-shirts printed, and made sure the money raised paid for the electricity bill, expenses, and wages before actually helping the pig; if they bothered at all. I know I do not sound in favour of charities, and I don't apologise for it. Of course, as I said earlier, there are many charities doing amazing things, and we work with them, but most of the experiences we have had have not been great, and we see flaws in them that just don't exist in a social enterprise model.

One thing we desperately need is animal sanctuaries so that if we do get opportunities to rescue animals, we have somewhere to take them. But they don't always work well as charities, and many of them have to close. So how would a sanctuary operate as a social enterprise? The thing that jumps right to my mind is the idea of offering the sanctuary as a destination for the public to visit and get involved in the animal care. The animals who would be kept there would have been rescued and so need food, shelter, care, and some love, so why not open the place up to encourage the public to visit and see how animals should live in peace and safety. Schools could visit and interact with the animals, and the children would be shown exactly what they eat and hopefully make some connections. On top of this, merchandise could be sold, and a small, simple coffee shop on site would be a good idea to get more out of each visitor. The coffee shop could be tendered out to another business to take on and run, so the pressure is off the sanctuary. The shop could sell other peoples work and products and operate on a sale or return basis so no stock has to be purchased. Part of the land could be rented out as allotments and vegetables could be grown and sold in the shop and even delivered locally. These are just some ideas, and we could think of many more. The key is to run the sanctuary but think outside the box about how to make it earn money and become sustainable. But, if it just operated as a charity relying on donations, it has fewer options to survive.

A social enterprise can still ask for donations and offer sponsorships for individual animals, but if the core costs can be covered by running as a social enterprise business model, it just makes much more sense and gives more time for the animals. With the costs covered, any donations can be used to help even more animals and grow the enterprise. I know I would happily pay to visit a sanctuary and spend time there and we see this model working in Phuket Thailand with elephant sanctuaries.

On a smaller scale, you could start your own social enterprise from your own home. Make Vegan products and sell them at weekend markets and use the profits to help the animals or to create a wage to get you out of a job that holds you back from committing to more activism. Selling ethical Vegan products means you will no doubt get the opportunity to talk to many people about Veganism and the benefits of it. Selling Vegan products in a booming market so is a very smart move right now. Starting a small enterprise in your part-time might lead on to bigger things and shouldn't be underestimated; many of the huge businesses have started this way. If you get your products and audience right, you could end up growing your small enterprise to give you all the money and time you need to make a real difference for the animals and our planet. Instead of borrowing lots of money or looking for investors, start with what you have and do something extraordinary with it. When you make some money, put it back into the enterprise and keep growing slowly and strongly with no risk and no debt. Once you get to the point where the enterprise is paying you a full-time wage, you have the chance to go all in and do what you love!

One great example of a social enterprise you could start at home is a Vegan cake business. You could make cakes and bakery produce and sell them privately, to other shops, and at markets and fairs. Use a percentage of the profits to fund an animal project or donate it to a particular charity who you know is doing a great job. We wrote a book all about this called 'Start A Vegan Cake Business' so check it out if this appeals to you.

Of course, there are many traps and pitfalls involved in running any business or social enterprise, but if you are suited to the entrepreneurial lifestyle and feel like this is for you, then give it a go! We started a previous bakery business with just £500 and grew it to the point where we were turning over £250,000 per year, and in five years we sold over a million products. This wasn't a social enterprise, but the principles of business are the same and we grew it like any social enterprise might grow. Be patient, work smart and hard, and keep moving forward learning from mistakes and not making them twice!

Starting a Social Enterprise is a big deal and can take a lot of time and work to make it successful; sometimes. It can take years and sometimes it can never work at all. I love the social enterprise model, and the idea that we can run our own business that is set up to benefit others is something that really appeals to us, and maybe it appeals to you too?!

CHAPTER 23

PUBLIC SPEAKING

"All the great speakers were bad speakers at first."

- Ralph Waldo Emerson

When you stop and think about all the people who have influenced you to Go Vegan - or influence you to do anything really - what methods did they use? For me, lectures and speeches definitely stand out as one of the most powerful mediums that have changed my mind and encouraged me to look at the world differently. Right away when I think about Veganism and Compassion, I think of Gary Yourofsky, James Aspey, and Karen Armstrong. Their speeches and public talks inspired me to look at my impact on the world and research further into a world I never realised existed. Their encouragement and passion drove me to take action, and I believe we all have it within us to inspire other people to act too.

Public speaking is only something I've done very few times and mostly in schools. The most recent was when we visited a private school in Phnom Penh, Cambodia to talk about kindness to animals and highlight the suffering they experience in the pagodas and on the streets there. We talked about compassion and encouraged the children to respect animals and be kind to them. We asked them to tell their parents if they ever saw anyone mistreating an animal or if they ever saw an animal who was injured or sick. This simple one-hour activity with children aged 4-5 was very effective, and I hope they will remember what they learned. If we can just plant this seed of compassion into young minds like these, then we can certainly reduce animal cruelty and cultivate the crops into a future Vegan harvest!

But public speaking isn't for everyone. It is terrifying! I can happily go into a classroom environment and talk to students but the idea of talking at an event or at an open mic night really puts me on the defensive. I was scheduled to speak at a Nerd Night event in Phnom Penh, but because I submitted my photo after the deadline, I didn't get to talk. I was relieved but also felt bad because I had an opportunity to speak out for the animals and didn't take it. I failed them and myself.

Now I realise my weaknesses and strengths, and for the time being, I am focussing on my strengths. I know from talking and writing and making videos, we do help people Go Vegan so I am growing that side of our activism before we explore something that we may not be as effective at. However, I do plan to face my fears and get involved in public speaking in the future and with this book and others published and in the pipeline, I know I have to promote them in as many ways as possible if I want to have the biggest impact for the animals.

If public speaking is something you are good at, then I urge you to do it as often as you can. Having the stage and a confident voice to get the facts across to people is priceless. If you haven't spoken publicly before but want to get into it, then perhaps you could practice by making YouTube videos giving a presentation or talk and then send that video to venues and events asking them to give you some time on stage. Start small, maybe at schools and colleges, and build up to the point where you can talk to large audiences.

Other things you can do is join a local speaking group that helps its members develop the skills required to deliver great speeches. Look at people you admire online and break down what they do in their talks. How do they hold attention? How do they pace their talk? What do they do that makes them so effective? Of course, you can't copy or mimic these people as we all have our own way of talking and our own personalities, but you can gather tips and tricks that will help you develop your speech or talk.

Taking time to practice has to be the number one tip for any speech. When you have written your speech, practice it on your own, then with your partner, then maybe add a couple of friends or family, and slowly build up the audience. Use the same speech over and over again and use the time practising to tweak and hone it, so it delivers perfect timing and ultimate impact. While you may think the speech is re-petitive to your ears, the people you deliver it to will most often be totally new to it. Think of it like a comedians per-formance. They go on tour and give the same fifty minute set with the same jokes, pauses, timing, and actions. They per-form their set hundreds of times and tweak it to get the most laughs.

We can approach our speeches in this manner and while we are talking about comedians, don't be afraid to add hu-mour if that's who you are. Animal Rights is a serious issue, but we can reach different people by approaching the subject in different ways. Humour can break down barriers and get people thinking about things they might otherwise never have thought about. Humour is powerful when done cor-rectly, and I always say to use your skills to deliver the mes-sage in your own way. Whether you are an artist, photo-grapher, comedian, acrobat, or performer, there is always something unique that you can bring to the fight for animal rights.

So get creative, be braver than I am right now and take centre stage to deliver the animal rights message that is boiling up inside of you!

CHAPTER 24

CREATE A DOCUMENTARY

"The most important word in filming is 'why'."

- Jean Reno

With the advancement of mobile phones, cameras, and social media, creating a documentary is pretty much open to anyone with a smartphone, a laptop, and a Facebook account. Documentaries can be on anything at all, so if you are interested in a particular area of Veganism and animal activism, then why not create a film to highlight the issues to other people? Your documentary can be as long or short as you like, and you can create it in any style. There are many guides and tutorials online to help you get started, but really, all you need is an idea, some creativity, and passion to get it made.

Your documentary doesn't need to be produced by any large organisation and you don't have to submit it to anyone. Simply post it on your social media accounts and ask your followers to share it if they like it. The power of the internet allows for good content to reach millions of people with zero investment! Of course, this is rare, and the chances of it happening are slim; but it can happen so why shouldn't it happen to your content? The one thing that is certain, though, is that if you never make anything, you won't have any chance of getting your message across to people. We posted a very short video about the dog meat trade in Cambodia and it reached over 80,000 organically. So if we have the right footage and people are interested in it, we can reach many people with no investment and no paid advertising.

When you start gathering footage, interviews, b-roll, and information for your documentary, you will find that you start to collect a vast library that can be used to create lots of micro-content. Short 30 second videos, quotes for memes, photographs, and audio. You can create trailers for your upcoming documentary and set a launch date to build up to. During the build-up, post related content to get people interested and keep drip feeding this content a couple of times a day on your social media platforms. Your audience will grow as a result, and you will start to peak peoples interest. With a larger audience, the chances of your documentary being shared wider are higher and the more people that watch it, the more people will be affected by it, and in turn, the more animals will be helped.

If you have no idea where to start but want to, then you can start your research by looking at short documentaries you like or ones that have appealed to you and held your attention. What was it about them that did this? What layout and format did they use? Was there a presenter or just a narrator? There is nothing wrong with taking inspiration from your favourite documentary makers and even using their methods. Of course, plagiarism is unacceptable and unnecessary, but there is nothing wrong with copying a successful model and using it to layout your story with your footage and information.

We started to make a documentary about the Dog Meat Trade in Cambodia and gathered so much footage that we put together a six-month campaign instead. As we travelled and made connections, we met new people and teamed up with them to work on other projects. Together, with our new friends and activists, we are using our six-month campaign and translating it all into Khmer so we can deliver the message to the people who actually eat the dogs and their networks. If we can work on the areas of health, compassion, Buddhism, and the environment, we can reach people and affect demand for a product. Then we use the original campaign to try and help people to make the connection that dog meat is no different to cow meat. So our footage that started as a documentary now has two campaigns that have sprung from it. One tackling the supply and demand in the country, and the other focusing on the global vegan animal rights message.

Creating an animal rights documentary is exciting, fun, adventurous, but also scary, sickening, and at times, should destroying. After witnessing a slaughterhouse where over 600 animals were killed, I was at a very low point for some time. But I knew this wasn't about me and kept working through it. I made sure to keep talking about what I saw and grew close to fellow activists who I shared the experience with. This is very important. Don't let the footage you see and the feelings you experience take you away from the goal of your documentary. You are doing this for the animals, nothing else, so stay strong, make sure you have a network of people who you love and trust, and keep talking and sharing your emotions and feelings with others.

One thing I am very passionate about is the idea that the footage of animals suffering will make someone money. This is why we chose not to give the footage to some international charities who only wanted to use it to raise awareness in the UK (translated to raise money). I talk about this in the Volunteer section so won't repeat it here. Of course, we are set up as a social enterprise, and the attention this documentary and campaigns bring will grow our audience, and our audience may buy our book (even this book) or click on an affiliate link like the Amazon products we advertise. But the documentary isn't being sold and none of us who filmed it or experienced it will be paid. No one sponsored the equipment, travel, or marketing costs of it and every penny spent came out of our own pocket and personal money and in future (when our social enterprise makes money) we will use profits from sales to do more of the same thing and also support other activists around the world.

Documenting what we see and what is really happening to the animals is a major task that is necessary if we are to show the world the truth and give them an insight into the cruelty and death they are paying for. We can all do this to some degree, whether it be a full-blown researched documentary or attending an animal slaughterhouse vigil. When the truth s shared on a massive scale by millions of people, that's when change can happen. Be part of this change and use your skills to show the truth and help the animals.

CHAPTER 25

START A BLOG

"If I waited for perfection I would never write a word."

- Margaret Atwood

Starting a blog might not sound like a form of activism, but when you have your own space to write and publish articles, without any interference from outside sources, you can write about issues that are important in the Vegan world. When you've published your articles on the website (which is really all that a blog is) you can share them on social media and get them infant of lots of people. At first, and without concentrating on search engine optimisation (SEO), you will find that no one visits your website. It's like opening a shop on the quietest street in the world and not telling anyone about it; no one will visit. But once you start writing articles consistently and frequently, employing some SEO, and sharing on social media, over time you will start to see the number of visitors grow. With some patience, persistence, and positivity, in a year or two, you will have a decent following. We found that at first, we had maybe five visits a day, and after ten months, that grew to fifty visits a day, but after eleven months, it went up to one hundred, and after twelve months we are flirting with one hundred and fifty. So it seems to grow rapidly once Google bots pick up that you are publishing frequently, but as we have read and now experienced, it takes at least a year to start growing rapidly.

We use a WordPress site, but not the free version. We chose to self-host because then we have full control of the content, and can add any links we like including advertisements with Google Adsense. Our self-hosted website is our central hub around which we have built our Epic Animal Quest. Self-hosting allows you to have your own specific .com or .whatever domain name which is important. The free version of WordPress doesn't allow for this, and it also controls plugins, themes, and layouts. There are many websites available to buy domain names and self-hosting packages and with some time and a few YouTube tutorials, its pretty straightforward to do yourself. If you don't fancy creating a full self-hosted website, then the free WordPress will do the job, but if you plan to grow and monetise it, then self-hosting is the only way to go.

For SEO, a plugin called 'Yoast SEO' takes care of everything you need to make sure your articles read well and are optimised for search engines. It's free, easy to use, and it gives you a score for each article and even shows you what to change or improve on. The red, amber and green scoring system is simple and very effective in letting you know where you can improve. Aim for the green light, and you can't go wrong!

We combine our books with our blog and write articles based around the niche we write the books for. This means we can spend a few months on a theme and end up with a rough draft of various chapters and ideas that can be expanded on and polished to form the makings of a new book. Each blog post article is signed off with a selection of links to our social media pages and links to buy a book or find out more. Including links throughout the article, that take readers to other relevant articles, is also a great idea to keep people on your website and keep them reading about the issues you feel are important.

Word count is a consideration, and anything of three hundred words is good. Recently, we trialled posting the full article text from our blog onto Facebook posts along with the link to go back to the website. This really helped the number of website visits we now get and was a great idea and recommend that we saw online when watching one of Gary Vaynerchuk's videos on YouTube. Gary Vaynerchuk is a New

York entrepreneur and marketing genius who has an awesome channel on YouTube. If you want to get some marketing advice, or just want to get your articles in front of more people, then Gary Vaynerchuk is the guy you need to be listening to.

Once your blog is up and running and you are posting articles regularly, you might want to think about monetisation. This can be done in a number of ways. You can register with Amazon to become an affiliate and then if you link to their products, you get a commission form any sales that are made. You can also use Google Adsense to bring in some revenue from ads placed exactly where you want on your site. If you have written a book, then include the link to your book and also make sure to use the Amazon affiliate link so you get paid for the book sale and the affiliate commission too. You could set up a YouTube channel and link that to your website and Adsense, and once you get over ten thousand views, you can start getting a small revenue from that. The idea with making money through a blog is to have lots of different income streams so that if one company like Amazon affiliates, or Google Adsense change the rules and benefits, you won't be left with the income you've gotten used to.

If you decide to write a blog, then you might as well use these things to bring in an income that you can use to either boost your social media posts or use it to help the animals directly. Making decent money from a blog takes time, and sometimes that can be many years. Lots of people quit early on because they don't see any return, but the great thing about writing a blog about Veganism and animal rights is that it doesn't matter if you get paid or not, it's being written for the cause, not the reward! We are creating our income around our books and then have all the other methods in place because it makes sense to do it, but we are not motiv- ated by money, and I would continue to do it whether we got paid or not. The first year of our blog saw us earning just £50 from Adsense, £5 from YouTube, and $750 from book sales. So after working almost every day, creating content, writing blog posts, articles, books, making videos, editing photos, and drawing cartoons, we didn't even make $1000!

This may seem ridiculous, but the revenue won't come in immediately. However, what you have written will exist as long as the internet does, so once it is out there, it has the potential to always bring you in an income. Books are pretty much immortal too, and if you write an evergreen topic, then you can sell all year round and continue to sell for years to come. To make a real income from this, the key is to get a lot of web visits each day. This can be done by patiently building your audience, or it can be done by paying to pro- mote and advertise on social media and other avenues. We chose the free, time-consuming approach, and have been working freelance and in contracted work to subsidise what we do. After a couple of years, your web visits will grow organically, and you will notice that Google searches go up quote rapidly, white quickly when you publish a lot of articles. We chose to post one per day, so we have written many articles so far and will continue to do so. In fact, we are scaling up and want to do at least two per day from now on.

Just like a book, you can write about any subject and get paid to make a living out of it, so why not write about what you are passionate about and use your writing skills to help the animals? You are not asking people for donations, and you are not asking other activists to fund your activism, you are asking them to buy a book that they want or need and if they don't do that, all you ask is that they read your website (if they want to and it interested them) and click on a few of the links if it appeals to them; this costs them nothing but puts you in a position to do so much for the animals and grow your audience.

Once you have a blog, and then write one or more books, you can start taking in part in public talks or school and college visits and pass on your written word in another way. Once you become known and get more and more coverage, you might well be in an amazing position to get your message out to thousands, even millions of people! This has to be one of our goals, and the more people who speak out like this, the better chance we have of someone breaking through and reaching many people with the Vegan message and animal issues.

CHAPTER 26

START A VLOG

"The most dangerous thing you can do is play it safe."

- Casey Neistat

I remember procrastinating for months before I finally made the decision and started Vlogging! I knew that if we want to make a difference for the animals then we had to share our ideas and thoughts and link up with other like-minded people to try as many different things as we could. The more people who come together and focus on a common goal, then the more chance we have of achieving it.

The process of making small movies that capture moments and memories can be enjoyable and coupled with the gadgets and equipment that you can use, it can build into a great hobby. Even making a video about just walking to din-

ner with our dog Alfie was fun to make, and we will always
be able to watch with fond memories and remember our
time in Phnom Penh and, our favourite restaurant there, The
Vegetarian. This is something that can build into a novel approach to vlogging and documenting your life in film. Make
it about creating memories for you and your children, and
especially future generations, and the videos and blogs soon
become a time capsule that you can treasure forever. Approaching it in this manner helps to forget about who is
watching (though we should always keep in mind that our
videos are for the viewers to be entertained or informed) and
lets you concentrate on what you are doing and allows you to
be yourself.

Vlogging is a great way to document your adventures
and leave a record for your children and the next generations
to look back and see what you did. What an amazing resource it will be in 50 years time, to look back at our lives and
know we did the right thing! Legacy is a big deal for me, and
I want to leave the world better than I found it. At the very
least I want to stop being part of the biggest threat to it and
reduce the harm I cause to the Earth and all the animals
who live on it. Will we succeed? Who knows, but if we don't
try and make the world a better place for our children, then
what does that say about us?

The videos and the content have to appeal to other
people. If you can incorporate some information and ideas

so that anyone interested in Veganism will want to follow you and learn more, then you have succeeded. If you choose to travel to places and document your adventures, then you immediately one up a whole new niche audience. There are thousands of niches that you can appeal to and so whatever you are in to and whatever adventures you embark on in your own life, I am pretty sure there will be people who want to watch. For our Epic Animal Quest, we chose to travel and show everyone just how easy it is to live Vegan pretty much anywhere in the world. We don't vlog very often now though and focus more on our books, but we do make videos about people and other animals we meet and our time with them.

Vlogging is a great way to share stories about animals and people while showing a real behind the scenes look at what we are doing and why we are doing it. If the video is a bit shaky or the cuts aren't crisp, does it really matter when the message is the most important thing? I think Vlogging allows for a more rough and ready approach to documentation and sometimes, to catch a special moment, you just have to whip out the camera and film from any angle you can.

Making videos and vlogging is all about sharing ideas and stories, and if we can find unique little stories in our day to day lives that promote animal rights and Veganism, then that is an awesome thing to do. Although gadgets and equipment are fun, all we need to convey these stories is a basic camera capable of video recording or just our smartphones. We can even edit videos on our, so we don't need a laptop or computer with fancy programs. Of course, better equipment and programs maker better-looking shots and edits, but if the story is strong, the quality can come second place. If you can get a great story across in an awesome way using the best equipment, then even better, but the barrier of entry based on equipment is a false one.

When you start out, grab your phone and find a quiet room and practice on your own. I found I could barely speak when I first started talking to the camera, and phone and the cringe level was high. After a while and after a few days of practising, I got more and more comfortable. I set myself a goal of making one video a day for 100 days and posted on Facebook that I was doing it. This made me accountable and meant I had to do it! After 100 videos, I improved but also found that this wasn't something I wanted to do every day. My passion is writing so I have to be true to that.

Just because we might initially be uncomfortable doing something like a Vlog, doesn't mean we shouldn't. The hardest part is just to start, just to go for it and give it a go! Standing in front of the camera and then watching and listening to yourself while you edit the footage is a very weird and narcissistic thing to do. I noticed my face was wonky, my voice sounded strange, and my expressions were all over the place, especially when I drank too much coffee! I never realised my face and erratic arm movements were so animated.

But once you get past these new discoveries - and this really doesn't take long to do - it actually starts to become fun. Talking in the streets as you walk along when there are lots of people around is something that I personally haven't built up to yet, but finding a quiet Pagoda to walk around or a quiet part of a park or building or even just sitting in front of my desk, is pretty easy. You can find somewhere you are comfortable with and then get practising.

Vlogging is a good way to start making videos because it follows the idea championed by Gary Vaynerchuk - a CEO of Vaynermedia, a giant marketing company in New York - of 'documenting not creating'. When you Vlog, you are essentially just talking to the camera without a script or without having to create any backdrop or props or even graphics. Your surroundings are your stage, and you can do it on your own or include the people you are with or meet during filming. It's spontaneous and requires little planning to execute. You can take advantage of this method to talk about issues around Veganism, and even just a walk in the park can turn into a philosophical discussion about moral and ethical issues.

When you are used to the vlogging format, you can branch out and start making different content and include graphics, photographs, and other video clips that are presented with you as the narrator. Many YouTubers like The

Bitesize Vegan, take this approach. It can be more time consuming as it requires much more planning and preparation and especially more editing, but the finished piece can serve as a powerful educational tool if you get it right. If you like giving presentations and can use Powerpoint or Keynote, then you can create awesome Powerpoint presentations around a topic and talk over the slides as it plays. Videos I like to make are around individual animals and their stories. I tend to use subtitles to narrate and play compelling music in the background. With the right story and music combination, these videos can really connect with people and create some interesting responses. One other option is to film a podcast where you talk about a set number of topics or just freestyle and see where the conversation takes you. You can do it on your own, but this format works well with partners or guests.

Duration of videos is up to you, but it depends on the content and the platform you share it on. Vlogs are generally around 5-10 minutes long, and that duration works for most platforms. Powerpoint presentations can be as long as you can hold the audience and the subject matter will have an influence, but they can be as short as one minute or as long as a documentary. For Facebook, one to three minutes works well right now, but we are noticing long-form content creeping in and starting to do well. YouTube seems to be an established place for the longer content such as documentaries, long presentations, and especially podcasts. The short stories that I like to make are well suited to Facebook and keeping them short at one to three minutes, works really well. IGTV is another option now, and videos can be longer than the minute allowed on Instagram.

It is important to match the content to the platform, so if you choose to focus on Facebook, think about what works best there and keep up to date with current trends. It's a good idea to follow pages and pool who are doing well and see the style of content, duration, and graphics they are using. Obviously, don't copy them, but use them as an influence to help you create your own style and put together content that stays on trend so you can get it in front of as many people as possible. Even when focussing on one platform, it is still good practice to share across all of the ones you use. That way, if one platform changes something or shuts down, you still have all your content online somewhere else. If you have a website or blog, be sure to share your video in a blog post which really helps with search engine optimisation.

Vlogging is a powerful way to get your message out into the world and connect with people. Combining it with other forms of activism like the slaughterhouse vigils and pretty much any activism activities you are taking part in shows people your perspective and may encourage them to get involved and do some activism themselves. All in all, vlogging is fun, it helps the movement, and once you get started, you might find you won't be able to stop!

CHAPTER 27

START A PODCAST

"With radio, the listener absorbs everything."

- Bob Edwards

Starting a podcast is something we never thought we would do but it has so many benefits, and when we tried it, we really enjoyed doing it! With voice and audio being predicted as the next big thing - we are already seeing 20% of all Google searches being performed by voice - we have to put ourselves in a position where our content is accessible to people in the way they want to consume it. We also want people to find us when they use voice and software like Alexa and Siri. So a podcast is perfect for this. People can discover audio content about Vegan issues and access it quickly and then listen to it on the move in their cars, while walking or at the gym. With short audio content, we can provide answers to questions that will suit the medium used.

Using an app like Anchor allows us to publish to the leading platforms like iTunes and have our podcast in as many places as possible to reach different audiences. Anchor makes it quick and easy to upload to and makes the job of distribution something you don't have to spend hours on. Of course, you still have to share links and get the attention of your followers pointed towards the platforms, but the hardest part is done for you. Anchor allows you to focus on creating the content and sharing the links to it. Find the app in the usual places for android and apple or visit them here at www.anchor.fm

There were a few insecurities we had when we started to make videos and podcasts. What will people think? How will we be perceived? We asked ourselves if we were too old or uncool to be on YouTube - obviously, this is silly - and cringed when we listened and watched ourselves. But all these things are just us being insecure, and I think it is natural anytime we start something new. Being uncomfortable is nothing compared to the what the animals go through, and anything worth doing rarely come easily or without discomfort and effort. So we dared to do, and started our podcast!

The idea that no one is listening is a strange concept when you first start your podcast. We produced our podcasts and although we thought people weren't consuming what we were saying, sharing the links to YouTube and Anchor and the videos themselves on Facebook, got the content in front of people and some listened! The day after our third podcast, we heard from a friend who we met in Phnom Penh who told us he is now Going Vegan! This is amazing, and for us, this is what it's all about. This one person will now not be responsible for the death of 400 animals per year and is even going on to create his own videos about Veganism and the importance of it to the animals and our planet. Imagine if we can help 100 people Go Vegan? Then they each help another 100 people. The numbers will be staggering and will make a very real difference to the number of animals needlessly killed, land needles destroyed, ocean habitats needlessly wiped out, and health unnecessarily damaged. So when you think no one is listening, put that idea out of your mind; you only need to connect with one person to make a difference!

Doing the podcast together was a bit weird at first, and we rarely sit down for an hour at a time and just talk without being interrupted by the kids. But the podcast allows us this time together, and it helps us to focus on particular Vegan issues and research more than we might have before. Because the format is relaxed, the kids can still talk to us as we create the content and can join in too if they want, making it a family activity. I don't know if we will do more family podcasts, but it was worth exploring. We will for sure be adding more audio based on our blog where we talk about the issue in each blog post, so look out for that!

One thing I didn't expect was the amount of content we got from the podcast. We could take a one hour podcast and create 10 or more shorter videos from it. Then from those, we could pull out 30-second quotes that worked well on Instagram. You can plan your podcast so that you cover a set number of topics and then use each topic as a separate video. Take the quotes and create memes with your photos for extra content for Twitter, Pinterest, Facebook, and Instagram. Podcasts are perhaps the best way to start creating content as they give so much in return for the time and effort given. You don't even have to be good at video or editing; just roll the camera and talk to each other!

When we started our podcast, we kept asking ourselves, how can we add value to the people listening? We asked, will this podcast actually help animals and are we in a position to give advice as we have only been Vegan for two years? Of course, all of us can offer advice and can certainly give our perspective and tell our own stories. Once we know better, and we learn about the benefits of Veganism, we are morally obligated to speak up and be outspoken for the animals; no matter how long we have known what really happens to them.

Each one of us is unique, and so we all have something different to offer the world. We can all talk about the same subjects, but we can also all give our own spin on them. Our personalities are what make people tune in and take notice of what we say, and because we are all so different, we will appeal to all different types of people. As Rachael and I are not young and cool, we probably won't appeal to young cool people, but will what we say be of interest to other parents who have young children and want to go Vegan and maybe travel? You bet!

Our goal with our podcasts was to keep it real. We wanted to come across as the normal people that we are and show people that anyone can go Vegan and live a happy and awesome life without animal products. Since we went Vegan as a family, we have never been happier, even though we have seen some horrific things. But if we can share our story, and answer questions other new vegans might have to help them transition easier and quicker, then that's our job now. If we can help people go vegan, stay vegan, and get active in activism, then we will be meeting our goals and making a difference for the animals; and so can you!

CHAPTER 28

ANIMAL SAVE MOVEMENT

"It's not whether animals will survive, it's whether man has
the will to save them."

- Anthony Douglas Williams

All across the world, people are forming Animal Save groups.
These groups have been made famous by the Toronto Pig
Save group who saw their member getting arrested and
charged for giving water to a thirsty pig inside one of the hot
transport vehicles. The actions of the group and the publicity
that followed have inspired many people to start their own
group or join an existing one. The Animal Save meetups are
peaceful and are there to bear witness to the animals. By
showing the world what really happens and putting a face to
the burgers and bacon, we hope that people will wake up
from their meat coma and realise they are eating sentient
beings that love, grieve, and fear just like we do. I talked

about the AnimalSave movement in a previous chapter, but not all vigils are part of this network, and you can take part without having to donate or be made to feel like you have to.

I attended my first Animal Vigil in Bodmin, Cornwall, with the Cornwall Animal Rights group who weren't affiliated with Save movement. I felt apprehensive on the journey to my first meeting and the previous night, Rachael and I watched some videos of other animal vigils across the country on YouTube to give me an idea of what went on. As I had never been to a Cornwall Animal Save vigil before, I wanted to try to prepare myself. Just watching those videos was very emotional but I imagined it would be nothing like being there in person and seeing the poor animals for myself. I was right. The experience was really strange, and reminded me of the feeling I had when my dog was taken to be put down at the vets. It was like attending a funeral for hundreds of souls but you saw them alive and walking into the crematorium themselves. Knowing that I could do nothing to stop their inevitable death was awful and seeing them stuffed into the trucks was heartbreaking.

My second vigil with the Cornwall Animal Save group was much more poignant than my first. It was evening and winter in the UK at the time, and the darkness, along with the cold, wet, and cloudy weather, made the place appear even more murderous than it did during the day. The atmosphere turned sinister as the evening went on and we started to hear the cries of the cows that were already inside. These weren't normal 'mooing' sounds in the distance, they were loud cries of terror and desperation that cut through me much deeper than the cold. Looking through the gates beneath the lines of barbed wire, I was helpless. Even if I did get into the compound, what would I do? If I managed to get a cow out of there, where would they have gone? I couldn't walk them down the road or take them home. The situation was pathetic, and so was I.

Getting over this feeling of helplessness is probably something that I will never do. But the vigils are not about me or you, it is about the animals. It is all about documenting the process and acknowledging the poor lives that are being taken needlessly and cruelly. Nothing about the system or procedure is humane, no matter how much meat eaters keep telling themselves it is. We want to be present and acknowledge that the cows, chickens, pigs, and sheep are living, breathing, thinking, feeling, loving, fearing, grieving, sentient beings. We see them at their final moments and try to express our compassion and love as best we can.

I hear many vegans saying that they couldn't cope with it and that they would get arrested and run into to save the animals or attack the staff there. The truth is they probably wouldn't do any of this. We all want to, of course, we do, but what good would it do? This is the time we all need to get over our own shortcomings and take some action. You don't have to be loud or confident to attend the vigils. I am not loud by any means and on my first meet up I really didn't say much at all. It just is a case of getting enough people together to attend the vigils, and then we will really have power in numbers. More people equals a bigger show of force, and that will bring more attention, more social media shares, more reporters, TV crews. More people will be shown the footage and realise the truth. They will make the connection and realise they are eating beautiful animals and not burgers. Before I was a vegan and even a vegetarian, I didn't make the connection. I am ashamed of myself and wish I had made it earlier than I did. I wish someone had shown me the reality and made me think about what I was a part of. The consumption of meat and dairy is the only reason these lives are being taken. If the market doesn't demand the animal flesh, then the animals will just not be killed. It's that simple.

During the vigils, we asked the drivers to stop for just 3 minutes. That's all. Just 3 minutes so we can film the animals, show our love and compassion, and mark the sad end of their poor miserable lives. Some stopped, but others tried to drive right through us. One of the activists actually got hit by a lorry at one of the meetups! Another time - I wasn't there but saw the video footage - a police officer opened their door into an activist, and she was knocked back into a moving lorry. She ended up with severe bruising o her legs and arms. This highlights the danger involved and shows the complete lack of humanity and compassion shown by the people involved. If the drivers and 'impartial' police force show this total lack of regard for human life, imagine how the throat slitters inside the slaughterhouses behave?

Some people will complain that the activists scare the animals; farmers are very fond of saying this. Being there and filming the animals seemed a little voyeuristic, and I can see why some people will say it is not fair to the animals to 'poke cameras in their faces'. The cameras show the reality. They show the condition of the animals and the ordeal they have to go through just to get a burger in a bun or a steak on the grill. The animals were already scared. They had travelled for hours in the back of a metal lorry or trailer. No food or water. No idea of where they were going or why. As the lorries drove by, the cows were poking their soft noses out of the gaps, and I could see their breath as it hit the cold air. As one driver engaged his gears and started to drive through the gates, the sound startled the animals, and you could hear their mooing increase in frequency and volume as they neared the unloading bay. I am sure they could smell the death all around them and could sense this was to be their fate too.

The process sees the animals frequently arrive, some in small trailers and others in large double lorries. They are soon unloaded right into the slaughterhouse with a gross efficiency, and not long after forklifts truck bring large crates of freshly peeled animal skin to a processing room. The slaughterhouse I attended had the crates covered up with large blue plastic sheets, which is something they wouldn't normally do. Since the Cornwall Animal Rights group have been documenting the process, a particular slaughterhouse, Merryn Meats, have been keen to shield the reality from the public.

I was able to film the heads and hooves and other animal parts that would not bring the farmer or the meat industry a profit. They were lifted up by a tipper and just poured into a skip. These beautiful animals are taken from a living breathing sentient being and stripped down to sandwich filings, burgers, and waste products. All this goes on while the drivers, security and slaughterhouse workers laugh, joke, smoke, and even eat their lunch of other dead animals.

The gate security and slaughter staff at these events mostly tend to keep their distance. The ones I met looked at us as if we were mad as if we were the strange ones. They laughed at us, smiled as they sharpened knives, and smirked when we were sad. After the events, there were a lot of comments on social media from the friends and family of farmers and slaughterhouse workers. All negative, vile, and idiotic, as you would expect. I had not been a vegan for very long, but I soon realised how savage people become when you stand up for justice and they don't want to stand with you.

There were Facebook posts with photos actually taken from the staff canteen in the slaughterhouse. The workers get cheap food as you might expect in any staff canteen, but this one gives cheap beef steaks. So the workers might spend their day slicing throats, tipping innards and heads into skips, sorting through skins or cleaning away the spilt blood, but during their break, they will also enjoy the dead flesh of the animals they have been killing all day. These people are perhaps lost to anything we could do to convince them this is wrong.

Compassion is completely void in these peoples lives and, unfortunately, I feel they will never change. The behaviour of the workers and the backlash on social media told me that the veil that has been pulled over societies eyes is a thick one. But this doesn't mean we can't stop this. Throughout history, minorities have risen up and grown to a tipping point where change can happen. Once that point is reached, it can happen quickly. All we have to do is keep working towards justice and speaking out for those that have no platform or voice of their own.

There are millions of people out there who will change and are changing every single day. You are one of these people who has changed, and now you have an opportunity to help others make to change too.

CHAPTER 29

EARTHLINGS EXPERIENCE

"Ultimately, we actually all belong to only one tribe, to Earthlings."

- Jill Tarter

I attended my first Earthlings Experience in Truro, Cornwall. Having watched lots of these street activism events on youtube, I had a good idea of what to expect going into it, but I still kept an open mind and decided to just see what happened on my first visit. We had a great turnout, lots of Cornwall Vegans attended (well great for Cornwall, there were around 12 of us) and we set up outside a large marquee where there was a ferret racing event and a farm animal show going on inside. Due to the location, we met a lot of farmers and even people who worked in the slaughterhouses. The thought of talking to farmers and slaughterhouse workers was not a positive one, but we were there to talk to anyone who was interested in what we were doing, and I was up for a challenge. I spoke to lots of people and was surprised to meet many vegetarians and vegans who balanced out the farmers. It was like opposite ends of the spectrum, those that didn't eat dead animals and those that raised and killed them, then ate them!

I came away from the evening feeling great, really positive. Attending the Cornwall Animal Rights slaughterhouse vigil events is very depressing, and you can often feel completely useless, but the Earthling Experience was totally different. People were interested in what we were doing and why we were there, and they stopped and asked questions and really engaged with us. Obviously many just walked by and the odd few sniggered or tutted, but overall, I would say that it was a really positive experience and would recommend it to everyone to try as part of their activism.

Being my first time at such an event, I used it as a practice to get used to asking and answering questions and seeing what the other activists did. After talking to one farmer for over 30 minutes, I had a good chance to go through pretty much every objection that veganism could receive! Trying to think of the answers I knew that I knew, quickly enough and in a logical way that was not confrontational took some patience. Obviously, I was fighting a losing battle, but I took the opportunity to answer a ton of questions, and who knows, maybe something got through to him.

Talking to the farmer gave me a chance to play some Vegan Bingo! In just 30 minutes I was able to go through the main objections to veganism like protein, tradition, lions, food chain, eating all the soy, countryside, what would happen to the animals, not healthy, etc. etc. I found we could go through all the objections and handle them one at a time, but as each one was handled, immediately another would be thrown in. Once we had gone in a big circle, it just started again! All the objections were brought up and repeated. This made for good practice, but I doubt any of the truth bombs hit their target.

If you are thinking of going along to take part in the Earthling Experience or other street activism, don't be put off by the idea that farmers will be there. I found this particular farmer to be alright to talk to, and he wasn't aggressive at all, though I did hear one or two others were getting a bit annoyed. Just remember, you don't have to talk to anyone you don't want to, so if you get someone's attention and you feel uncomfortable in any way, just thank them for stopping and then walk away. You will be in good company, everyone will support you, and the only pressure you will be under is that which you apply to yourself.

I think that when you are in the street doing this kind of activism, it's really important to be friendly, approachable, and polite. Going up to a complete stranger and getting into their personal space then asking them questions about their lifestyle could be seen as intrusive. If I steamed in with a serious face and told them they were animal murderers, then I don't think they would stop and talk. They would only leave with a bad experience and think all vegans were crazy. So after watching the other activists, I copied their polite and friendly approach and asked people if they had heard about The Earthlings Experience before. Pretty much everyone hadn't, and this sparked a little curiosity in some. This then gave me a chance to ask more questions and move towards things like the egg industry or the treatment of pigs. Not everyone is going to agree with my approach, and that's great, we need a mix of people and personalities just as in any other area of life.

We had the virtual reality headset and tried to encourage members of the public to try it. Many didn't want to, but a few did. After witnessing the life (and death) of a pig in the first person, you could see that people were affected by it. Some even had a few tears welling up. After talking to people and showing them the virtual reality or the video document-aries, some people thanked us for being there and thanked us for bringing the reality of the meat, egg, and dairy industries to their attention. Most of the people I talked to said they would go away and look into it more and the flyers we handed out to them directed them to the Vegan Society, Earthlings Documentary, Cowspiracy, and Forks Over Knives.

Even knowing the truth, some people will carry on re-gardless. What I found the most difficult was telling someone about things like the ocean dead spots and the idea that the oceans could be dead by 2050, and they already knew about it but still carried on eating fish and eating meat. It was really odd that although they knew the problems, they still didn't want to do anything to stop them and were happy to be a part of it. Even the idea that the future could be bleak for their children did not inspire them to change their ways or even look into the subject further. For some, the taste of fish fingers or beefburgers overpowers their desire for a bright future for the animals, themselves, their children, and the planet. It really is strange to hear from people.

Street activism has always been around with people protesting about fur or leather or even other social justice issues. The introduction of the Virtual Reality and the Earthlings Documentary has really given vegans an opportunity to get out and do something positive in their local area. The great news is that you don't even need the Virtual Reality, you just need a few people standing with laptops or tablets showing the documentary and a few people talking to passers-by. Flyers can be ordered free of charge or with a small donation from many Vegan websites. Some of the other activists write down links to websites and documentaries like Earthlings or speeches by Gary Yourofsky. This is a brilliant idea and one that I will be adopting in the future.

Following the Truro Earthlings Experience, we had had two reports of people going vegan. This was awesome news and showed us that this kind of street activism really does work. If we have heard of two successful cases, I wonder how many we haven't heard of? The more people that come along and take part in these events, the more people we can all talk to and educate. The more people we can point in the right direction and get started to research all the information for themselves, the more people will choose to go vegan, and, for the right reasons.

We are really in a position to make a change here. Imagine if every week, each one of us could talk to one person and get them to choose to go vegan? Then those new vegans could do the same thing the following week, and so on. How long would it take for everyone to go vegan or at the very least, for a large proportion of the population? Take 20 vegans in Truro, they each then get one person to choose veganism, then those do the same. Every week the number of vegans would double. Continue this doubling every week, and in just 32 weeks, everyone on the planet would be a vegan! This sounds crazy, and it won't happen like this, but the example of exponential growth is accurate, and it can multiply this fast.

If you are a vegan and can make it to an event like this, then pop along and join in! If you are interested in finding out more about being a vegan, then go along and talk to the people there. Most vegan Animal Activists I have met have been extremely friendly, and I know they would love to see you. Remember, if we truly want change to happen, we have to be willing to make a change ourselves and then get out there into the real world to engage with other people face to face. The change will not happen on a big enough scale just by having arguments with meat eaters online or by posting photos of our meals every day. Being a vegan is about so much more than this. Our children need us to do this so they will have a bright future ahead of them, the planet needs us to act now, and the animals need us to speak for them all around the world; they desperately need our help. Let's make this happen, let's change the world together!

CHAPTER 30

CHALKING

"Creativity is contagious. Pass it on."

- Albert Einstein

Chalking is something I haven't done yet and don't know if I ever will. The idea of adorning a sidewalk or a park path with vegan messages is appealing and something I guess I should do once to see what happens. I imagine that getting there early in the morning before everyone gets up to walk their dogs or take the trip to work and then cover a section of a path with colourful and thought-provoking messages could be effective. Would people read them and take them in, though? I'm sure they would and what a way to get the morning started!

This has been done with some effect outside of places like McDonald's and combined with an earthlings experience or cube of truth event, this gets attention, gets people talking, and certainly gets our points across; with a little healthy disruption thrown in for good measure.

The legalities of chalking should be checked in your area before going out and grabbing some chalk sticks and getting creative. If it's classed as graffiti, then you could be arrested, charged, or fined, so be mindful of that. The fact that it is easily washed away takes away the permanency of the act, and no damage is done to any physical property. So make sure you know what the consequences could be for you if complaints are made; which should be expected if chalking near businesses or in busy public areas.

I suppose that chalking wouldn't be good for people who have no artistic bones in their body but that said, anyone can give it a go if they can write, and you may surprise yourself! If you are not sure what to write or draw, then grab some ideas online and just copy what other activists have done. Plagiarism has no place in the animal activist chalking world, and I am sure everyone would be happy and flattered that their words and artwork were copied and used to further the message and help the animals.

Animal Rights quotes seem to me to be a good place to start, and I can picture a path covered in these thought-provoking and philosophical messages. Accompany them with a few drawings or quirky drawings, and you have the makings of a temporary billboard that people won't miss!

While we were in Thailand staying in Phuket near the fantastic beach at Kata Bay, we had the idea of writing messages and quotes in the sand. Getting up early and filling the beach with positive and thought-provoking messages seemed like such a cool idea and no damage would be done to a property so we could be completely safe to do it in a foreign country and as a family without worrying about being charged, harassed or arrested.

Once the chalking or sand writing is finished, photos and videos can be made that will have a much wider appeal and effect. Use the artwork to create inspiring posts for social media and even write a blog post about what you did for your website or websites like Medium.com. Sharing ideas about activism is key to getting more people active in animal activism and the more activists we have, the quicker we can increase the population of vegans and reduce the numbers of animals being mercilessly killed for food we don't even need.

Chalking will undoubtedly come under the section of Art, but I wanted to give a short chapter to it on its own as I feel it is something we can all do very easily and with no barriers to entry and minimal costs involved. When we get creative with our activism and conduct ourselves in a friendly and peaceful manner, we show a different side to the stereotypical form of activism that many people have in their minds.

For me, chalking conjure up images of the 1970's, colourful bubble writing and fun drawings being sketched out in parks and recreation spaces under the summer sun by groups of young cool kids with flowers in their hair! But it doesn't have to be something just for the youngsters to get into; we can all grab a stick of white chalk and jot down a few words. So give it a go, share your messages, and see how you can get unlikely people to read things they would never ordinarily be exposed to, then share it with the world!

CHAPTER 31

UNDERCOVER FOOTAGE

"The lifeblood of Mercy For Animals is our undercover investigations of animal agriculture."

- Nathan Runkle

This is something I never imagined I would ever be doing, especially in slaughterhouses around the world. While we were filming for our dog meat documentary in South East Asia, we realised how straightforward it can be to get into places we thought would be impossible; certainly in the UK where we came from anyway. We thought we should try to get access to other animals and the processes they go through too. Where we were at the time, there weren't that many barriers, and we were finding that if we spoke to the right people and got lucky, we could get access to things that we just wouldn't get access to in the West. Once we had that undercover footage, we knew we could share it and show what happens to animals, not just in Asia, but in every slaughterhouse in every country around the world. With the fences, gates, and guards removed, these slaughterhouses didn't have glass walls, they didn't have any at all!

In a few months, we managed to film cows, pigs, ducks, and dogs in slaughterhouses from small family run affairs killing one or two animals a day up to large commercial ones killing in excess of seven hundred animals in one night. It was awful, horrific work. Filming animals who were being killed while keeping our motives secret and being vigilant for our own safety. Sometimes, we had to film in secret and managed to find locations where a zoom lens would see right into the spaces being used to massacre so many innocent lives.

Watching animals being murdered and not having the power to stop it, is something that I will always feel guilty about. We watched dogs being drowned and didn't stop it. We watched cows being smashed over the head with an axe and stood still. We watched while pigs had their throats cut and kept rolling the film. For weeks after one experience, in particular, I hit a low point and spent hours in my own head questioning what we did and why we were doing it. Now, I've come to a place where I believe this footage will help change minds. If we can change enough of these minds, then we can prevent many of these killings and not just in the countries we filmed, but everywhere around the world. As I write these words and you read them, animals like these are still being killed every day and we have to work as hard as we can to stop it.

Some of our footage was too dangerous to post as our own, so we gave it to an international organisation who did an amazing job distributing it and using it to deliver the messages we wanted in the country or origin and globally. Other footage we use ourselves and have created campaigns around that will go on for many years to come. We know that the footage has made people change their mind and even Go Vegan because of it, so this is our consolation when we remember what we were part of. When we read some of the comments under the international footage, we could easily have been put back in that low place. One person said we were disgusting for filming it and not running and stopping it. But how could two or three of us run into a slaughterhouse and rescue seven hundred animals from fifty or so knife-wielding workers? Even if we did, where would we put the animals?

I think it's easy to make comments like that thousands of miles away, but even if we weren't there, those animals would have been killed in the exact same ways. The next night, it happens again, and on and on and on. Do we rescue seven hundred animals a night? Or, do we use the footage to affect supply and demand and then reduce those numbers each night? Comments like this make me sad to read, but I don't let it get to me if I can help it. The people making those comments also live near slaughterhouses, and they can illegally run into them and try and save hundreds of cows, pigs, chickens, and sheep if they really wanted to; no one is stopping them.

We just have to be realistic about what we are trying to achieve and the tools and methods we have to use to achieve it. If we can get footage of the reality of the meat and dairy industry and show people where the meat comes from - and who it comes from -and how these poor animals are processed from living, loving, sentient beings into slabs of flesh in a plastic wrapper, then we can reduce the demand and reduce the numbers of animals who are killed every day, everywhere.

One thing I feel very strongly about is the idea that no one should benefit financially from the footage. We were asked to give some footage to an international organisation so they could raise awareness in the UK (roughly translates to raising money) and they had no idea how to use the footage in the country we got it from. They did suggest using the footage to raise money and that some of that money would go to a local charity they support, but we knew the charity as we worked with them of six months and they explicitly said they didn't want any involvement in the dog meat trade. But they were happy to take the donations because of it, it seemed. As self-righteous as this might sound, I felt this was unethical, and we wanted nothing to do with it. So we chose to keep the footage and put it out ourselves and use our own money to pay to distribute it and get the message across. As our social enterprise gets to the point of making a profit, we will use the profits to do more of this work and support other activists who are in the same position that we were in.

Another idea was for the organisation to get the story in the UK newspapers, but all it would do would be to raise money for their organisation, and the bureaucracy would suck up most of it with little going to any work that would actually make a difference. We met with them a few times when they all flew out to South East Asia for capacity building and re-search, and they agreed to just share what we post. So that ended up being a good result with no one making money from the suffering of animals.

We made our decision to film what went on (and still does) in the slaughterhouses and then do everything we could to get that footage in front of the people who it will encourage to Go Vegan, Stay Vegan, and Get Active in Animal Activism to stop it happening. Seeing footage like this made us go vegan, and we believe it is important to get up to date footage from every country to prove to people it is real and not an isolated event.

Getting undercover footage is not for everyone. We were literally filming with tears rolling down our faces and hands shaking, but it is necessary. If this is something you have an opportunity to get involved with and feel like you can do it, then go for it, take care, make sure you are safe and stay that way and don't do it alone. We recommend checking the laws in your location and be aware of who owns the places you intend to film. Sometimes, especially abroad, there are issues of corruption and illegal activities, and if you are caught exposing them, you could get into serious trouble. It may sound extreme and exaggeratory, but this is the reality in some countries.

With some motivation, opportunistic behaviour, and outright luck, we can put ourselves in positions to be able to capture footage that can really make a difference for the animals.

CHAPTER 32

BUYING ANIMALS

"It's all about saving lives."

- John Hardee

In this chapter, I want to make a case for why I think there is a loophole in the common idea that buying live animals from slaughterhouses is a bad move. As animal activists, we are often forced to stand vigil and bear witness to animals as they are driven into slaughterhouses to meet their deaths by gas, electrocution, bolt gun, or knife. In some countries, methods include metal poles, the back of an axe, and drowning. We watch these animals, knowing that soon they will be cut up and packaged to be sold to consumers in shops and markets.

We know that choosing to go Vegan means fewer animals will be killed; or more specifically, fewer animals will be bred into existence to be killed to fill our stomachs. This is why we try to show the way animals are treated, the reality of the slaughter processes, and the impacts to health and environment in a bid to encourage others to go Vegan and spare more unnecessary sufferings and deaths.

But what if we had an opportunity to spare more life? What if we could save one of the animals who we see about to enter a slaughterhouse? What if we could stop the delivery driver and buy one of the animals from them?

Buying a live animal from any meat trade is frowned upon by the major animal charities and organisations. But why should their word be final? And from what I've seen so far, many squander money through inefficiency, inexperience, bureaucracy, and mismanagement. I found many to be more motivated by raising money than by solving the problem they are raising the money for. They are quick to lecture and criticise activists who actually save animals yet have little input or take little action in doing the same thing themselves. We are told that paying to rescue dogs from the dog meat trade is terrible, yet paying for people to travel across the world on capacity building, and research exercises are perfectly acceptable. While they have their meetings and dine using well using the money raised to solve a problem, activists are in the field and on the front line with the chance to save a life; and they are often there with no financial support from anyone! I can't be lectured like this and feel that I can make an argument that defends the choice to buy animals and save lives. We can't be told what to do by organisations who are not in the country and aren't acting in the country to stop the dogs being killed. We also will not listen to international organisations who are in the country but refuse to even speak out against the dog meat trade for fear of losing their Non-Governmental Organisation (NGO) status. The worst part for me is that these same organisations will use the dog meat trade as a reason for donors to give the money! It's totally gross, and these unethical people have no right to tell me that rescuing a life is wrong, especially when they are making money because of them.

This is a common message presented by the leading animal welfare organisations that state that buying animals only fuels the industry from which you buy them. The idea is that if we buy ten animals, the supplier will just get ten more and then maybe even breed or capture an extra ten in the future so they would be ready should you come back for more.

But what if you bought an animal right before they entered the slaughterhouse and you made it clear that you would not be back again in the future? What if you expressed clearly that this was a one time deal? The driver or supplier would not have time to go back and get another animal to replace the one you bought, and they would be happy to accept a price higher than that given to them by the slaughterhouse. They win, and so does the animal!

Saving one animal might sound great, but when there are 60 billion animals killed every year for the food we don't even need to survive and thrive, what difference does saving one life make? Aside from making a difference in one animals life, saving a young healthy animal who doesn't want to die, seems like the right thing to do; doesn't it? But ask yourself, what if you were that one animal? Would you want to be saved?

This reminds me of the trolley problem. Picture a train coming down a track with a junction ahead splitting into two tracks. On the right-hand track, there are 4 complete strangers tied to the rails. On the left, just 1 person is tied down, but they happen to be someone we love. If we do nothing, the train will carry on down the left track, and our loved one will be killed. If we switch the lever, however, the train will be diverted and will kill the 4 strangers. What do we do? Do nothing and let our one family member die, or switch the lever and let four total strangers die?

The trolley problem has been adapted to give an interesting alternative scenario that highlights an issue within animal rights. This time, it's slightly different. We have 4 animals - who we do not know - tied to the right-hand track. If we switch the lever, the train will be diverted and will go down the left-hand track. Now, here comes a twist. There are no animals on the left-hand track! If we do nothing, 4 animals will die. But if we choose to hit the switch, then we will save 4 animals, and no one else will be harmed!

We all have this choice to save lives every time we order from a menu or shop in a supermarket. Every small action or decision we carry out adds to the bigger picture. If all of us make small choices and opt for meat-free meals, then the difference would be enormous, and many animals would be spared sufferings and unnecessary deaths. We all have a switch and often the means required to take this further and pay to save a life. So what is stopping us?

After filming undercover footage at slaughterhouses and not stopping what was being conducted, I have to check my own motives. Would I be buying the animals to ease my own guilt? Watching animals die needlessly so we could collect footage to use in outreach or to highlight the cruelty and mistreatment is emotionally challenging, to say the least. The guilt gained from watching animals die while we stood aside and did nothing to stop it, created a mental battle that raged on for months after the events. So do we feel like we should buy an animal just to ease our own conscience? Perhaps, but we would still be saving a life nonetheless, and if we stick to the guidelines and make sure the delivery driver could not replace that animal and that we would not return to do repeat business, then what harm does it really do?

Even if buying the animal just eases our conscience, why is that so bad? A life will have been saved. I have to convince myself that our filming was necessary to use to save future lives, and that recording the deaths or standing vigil doesn't make activists complicit in the slaughter and being there might make the treatment of the animals better; at least while they are still in plain sight.

The idea that we can save a life if we pay for it seems terrible on so many levels. How much is an animals life worth anyway? A farmer would say the animal is worth the amount they sell them for less the costs of raising them. A domestic pet breeder would say the same thing. But what about a pet who we love? How much would we sell our pet for if selling them meant they would be concussed in some way and then have their throat cut before being cut up into pieces and fed to people? There would not be any price we would accept for this. Likewise, how much would we pay to stop it from happening? If our pet was stolen for the dog meat trade, and we could buy them back from the dog catchers, how much would we pay?

If we buy one animal who is destined for slaughter from a supplier or the delivery driver, and we can offer more than the price the animal would otherwise be sold for, are we not obliged to do it? We have set aside and hopefully even justified the idea that our action would fuel the trade, so going forward, why would it be so wrong? If we bought the animal from a supplier in a very poor country, we would be giving them more money for their family to live off for that day or week. The animals life is spared, the delivery driver can buy better food for their family; everyone wins.

If after this attempt to argue the case people are still against buying an animal to spare their life, let's imagine a purely hypothetical and philosophical thought experiment where the young animals we propose to buy are human toddlers. These toddlers would be killed and eaten if we didn't buy them. They weren't being held to ransom, and none of the workers or delivery drivers knew we were planning to buy any of them until they reached the end of their shift at the slaughterhouse gate. If we could buy just one child, and that action didn't make the supply chain, and it's agents produce or catch more toddlers, would we not be morally obligated to save that child and offer enough money needed to do it? What would the correct price be for a human child's life? Should we stop at one child? Why not buy all of them from the lorry if we could? Or should we listen to the international 'experts' and have a meeting about it instead?

Is doing something like this just one time enough? We know we can't save many animals like this and that the answer lies in reducing the demand for the dead animal's flesh. But if we get the chance, shouldn't we save at least one innocent life? If we know we can save the life, and believe that doing so won't fuel the trade and increase demand, do we really have any choice but to do it?

CHAPTER 33

ANIMAL LIBERATION

"Hope is the seed of liberation."

- Jon Sobrino

What does it mean to liberate an animal? Is it legal to do so? Is it safe? Taking an animal from a situation of harm to a safe environment is something that most people would imagine themselves doing - whether Vegan or not. A fireman will climb a tree for a cat or rush into a burning building to rescue a pet dog or rabbit. But when we apply this idea to a farm or slaughterhouse, all of a sudden we become extremists.

If we see an animal in distress, we have to act to do something about it, and we can't ignore suffering and abuse. But when we go onto someone's property to remove an animal that is classed in the eyes of the law as 'property' we cross a line from rescuing an animal to stealing one. This is why we can not tell you that this is a good thing to do, and you have to make up your own mind, do the research, and decide if it is something you can do and get away with. One organisation that is taking this and creating a movement around it is the Direct Action Everywhere enterprise. Direct Action Everywhere, is a donation based organisation working to build a global network of animal liberators. They organise events where volunteers act together to walk into slaughter-houses and farms and remove sick and injured animals. They also prepare to take part in civil disobedience to bring attention to the movement and try to make a difference for the animals.

We do not recommend this action nor can we endorse the donation based enterprise that the Direct Action Everywhere has become (because we know nothing about them and their accounting and measurement procedures), but it is worth looking at what they do, and then you can make up your own mind if this is for you or not. I know from first-hand experience how powerful it can be to work without an umbrella organisation or logo and form small groups with activists who receive no funding. There is nothing more empowering than working with a couple of people to do something that the large organisations will never do and then use that to reach thousands of people and help them make the connection. Affecting change doesn't have always to be done in this way with spokespersons and organisations. We can affect change as small pockets of activists using guerrilla-style tactics. But that said, we do need money to do things on a large scale, so perhaps this method is something to look at and perhaps the Direct Action Everywhere organisation is worth donating to, but in true effective altruism style, we should see the effectiveness and outcomes being measured and shared before we do.

Nevertheless, here is an excerpt from their website at https://www.directactioneverywhere.com/theliberationist/2015/1/9/on-the-importance-of-open-rescue-three-reasons-the-ar-movement-has-to-get-serious-about-liberation

"Our goal is to take open rescue across the country and world. If we truly believe what we say we believe -- that our lives are no more valuable than theirs -- then it's time for our movement to show that with our actions. That does not mean that every person can or should directly participate in an open rescue. Such investigations, if done properly, take months of effort, huge time commitments, and (though far cheaper than conventional investigations) thousands of dollars. If done poorly, they can lead to serious legal consequences, wasted resources, or, worst of all, harm to animals. But even if all of us cannot do open rescue, all of us can be part of a network that rescues animals from places of violence. Like all forms of nonviolent direct action, open rescue can only be born from a powerful community.

If the result of our action is just a temporary media blip, we will have failed in our duty to the animals. Mei, Sephy, and others will have been saved. But so many others were left behind. We cannot let their stories be forgotten. And that is why, today, we announce DxE's newest community project, the Open Rescue Network, and its four principal goals:

- To openly rescue animals from places of violence.
- To train and support others in doing the same.
- To document the violence inherent to animal slavery.
- To tell the stories of those who were saved.

Until Every Animal is Free. "

So do the research, figure out if the actions you take warrant the consequences, and decide if the consequences are something you can handle. Don't feel pressured to break the law and don't give in to peer pressure. If you get arrested, it may make the news headlines for a while, but when you are behind bars, you won't be doing any activism at all! There is much you can do without breaking the law and liberation can take place away from the cameras and social media coverage. If you feel like you can rescue an animal who is suffering then why only do it when the cameras are there? You could go out into the night when all is quiet and slip away unnoticed with an animal and no one every has to know about it. If discovered, on your own or maybe just a couple of you, you could plead innocence and say you are lost. If you don't break in, damage or disrupt, then you are only trespassing, and if you leave when asked, you may find the consequences will be much less. Stay safe, be smart, and always do what you feel is the right thing to do for everyone involved, including yourself.

CHAPTER 34

BOYCOTTING

"Passive resistance and boycotting are now prominent features of every great national movement."

- Benjamin Tucker

Boycotting is the easiest of all activism and the quietest. In fact, no one ever needs to know if you don't want them to, and they would not find out. You just simply choose not to buy one thing and buy something else instead. Of course, it's great to share what you are boycotting and why as it helps to show other people that a product is bad. Give the reasons why it's bad, show what happens to the animals to produce it, and even show some great ethical alternatives. Cleaning products are a great example. If we find a company that tests on animals, we can boycott all their products and encourage others to do the same. If enough people stop using the company and their products then they will have to cease trading or switch to products that people are demanding. Supply and demand is our biggest tool in combatting any animal product, and it's something we have to do in large numbers. So while it's cool to boycott on your own and keep quiet about it, it's much more effective to share what you are doing and encourage others to follow your lead.

There's not a great deal to say about boycotting, it is what it is, and anyone can do it. Once we decide to not spend our money on one thing but on another, we have a say about the economy. When we pay for something, we acknowledge it's worth and approve it. When we buy meat, we pay for the cruelty and murder of the animal and everything that poor animal experienced during their sad life. We endorse the farmer, slaughterhouse worker, and the butcher. We say that we think all the cruelty was worth 'x' amount to us and we thank them for doing it, When we refuse to buy something, we say the complete opposite.

So think of all the great Vegan products you use now and compare them to the old ones that you used to use. Perhaps you could write some blog posts or Facebook posts about the benefits all these new Vegan products bring you and the animals? Then share with as many people as you can. This is simple, easy to do, and it's not confrontational at all.

CHAPTER 35

STICKERS

"Once you label me, you negate me."

- Kierkegaard

Stickering is something that I have seen dividing people in the social media comments. Stickering is simply putting vegan animal rights messages on stickers and then sticking those stickers onto produce in the supermarkets or on anything where someone will read it. The hope is that people will see it and make the connection. A picture of Peppa pig on a pork chop, a photo of a baby cow on a milk cartoon or beef steak, and a photo of a baby sheep on a leg of lamb.

When people are reminded that what they are eating is not meat but the dead rotting flesh of a corpse that once belonged to a beautiful animal who didn't want to be killed, they may think twice about buying and eating it. But does it have a lasting effect and does it even work? I don't think we have any real evidence to say either way, but it does have good points and bad points.

If someone doesn't buy the food because of the sticker, then it is a victory. Less produced would be ordered to take its place, and if this happened often enough, the demand would go down, and the items wouldn't be stocked any longer if they didn't sell.

If the stickers are discovered by the shop staff and can't be removed, then the food is often thrown away and replaced anyway. This adds insult to injury as the food or flesh is not even used, so the animal died for absolutely no reason at all and another animal's body part or excretion will take its place.

Some activists see it as confrontational and wasteful and don't think it is worth doing. Sometimes, being controversial or confrontational is necessary, and we can't always be pass-ive. Our approach is passive in the way we share our lifestyle, but we are also on the offence of gathering footage, cam-paigning, boycotting, and disrupting. If stickering puts people off eating meat for one day then it has to be worth it.

If putting some stickers on meat and milk makes people up-set or angry then we have to ask why? Why are they so mad that someone has put a label showing them that it's not a happy chicken but a frightened, tired, confined, and abused one. Why not show them the chick grinding machine or what park looks like when it still alive?

Any activism that gets people talking, thinking, and question-ing has to be good and if our actions help to stop someone eating an animal - or has an effect that is positive for the animal without causing harm to anyone - then surely it has to be considered? We may not agree with it, but that doesn't mean it is wrong to do it, and if you feel like it's a good idea then go for it. The great thing about activism is that there are no rules. As long as no one is hurt (and this includes all animals including the human ones) by our actions, then we should be free to do anything.

CHAPTER 36

MARCH

"To sin by silence when they should protest makes cowards of men."

- Abraham Lincoln

Attending an Animal Rights March is one way we can show solidarity and that we mean business. When individuals come together in vast numbers to show that they demand change and that they are fighting for injustice, it is difficult to ignore them!

We have to speak out for the animals because no one is listening to them. When we speak out together as a large group, we are acting out of compassion and remaining peaceful while showing our numbers is a strong message to deliver.

Meeting other people, other Vegans especially is always awesome and gives us a reminder that we are not alone in this fight. There are millions of Vegans all around the world so getting a few thousand of them together in one place is always going to be a positive experience. You get to meet new people, make new friends, and network to build your contacts and possible collaborators.

Peaceful protests get attention, and the more attention, the better. When people see this is a serious subject being taken seriously by so many people, they look into, read up on the issues, and are generally exposed to those issues through the inevitable media coverage. If they act on what they read and learn, then perhaps they will be at the march themselves the next year!

Marches alone will not make the change, but attending and supporting them is something important we can do in addition to all our other activism. Social media has certainly had an effect on bringing groups and niches together, and it also makes organising marches and protests much easier. The temptation can often be to stay online but getting out and being surrounded by thousands of people who feel the same way you do is something that can't be achieved when on your own with your laptop.

If attending a march empowers and motivates people, those people can leave and go on to do amazing things. Often, it's just a catalyst for change and all people need is the push, and the permission to act. So join together with others, attend protests and marches, no matter how small they are, and show the world that we want to see a change and that we are no longer prepared to stand by and watch the torture, abuse, and death that is inflicted on animals every second of every day in every country around the world.

CHAPTER 37

HUNTING SABOTAGE

"A coward is incapable of exhibiting love; it is the prerogative of the brave."

- Mahatma Gandhi

This is something I have never done myself but want to next time we are back in the UK. Currently, it's illegal to hunt foxes in the UK, but that doesn't stop those with money from doing it! This sick, cruel, and cowardly blood fest is called a 'sport' by those that take part in it, and they even call it 'vermin control'. As Ricky Gervais says, 'the only way Fox Hunting would count as vermin control is if the posh twats fell off their horse and broke their necks," and I can't help agree with him. It couldn't be further from a sport, and this despicable animal abuse and murder of innocent defensive animals has to stop.

Sadly, even with the law on the side of the activists, fox hunting still carries on, and the police tend to turn a blind eye to it, and some officers have even been found to participate in it themselves when off duty. But it doesn't stop many brave, selfless activists going out in all weathers every weekend to stop it. They use tactics to put off the pack of hounds and try their very best to help the fox get away. With the UK recently making it law that animals aren't capable of feeling pain and removing them from sentient being status, it is only a matter of time until fox hunting is legalised again. It's like we are living in an alternate reality, how can this law have passed? How can a so-called advanced country like the UK make this decision and we have to ask who instigated it and who paid to make it happen?

If you are able to show support and join in this activism then you can find groups easily enough, so get involved and help stop these psychopaths from watching their hounds rip helpless animals apart for their own perverse pleasure and entertainment.

Another form of hunting in the UK is the badger culling. We attended a badger patrol in Devon when we lived in the UK and went out to look for badger traps, cages, and hunters. We made sure no hunting was happening on public land and looked for injured or trapped badgers so we could free them. By having a presence in and around the hunt areas at night, shining torches, making a noise, and generally being a warning to badgers to stay away, was all we could do. But it can be enough to save lives and prevent these morons killing these amazing animals.

Even with lobbying and protests, the badger cull continues and recently the UK government set plans to pay farmers £50 for every badger they kill in the ignorant fear of the spread of bovine TB from cows to badgers. Culling has now been rolled out to areas that are low risk, and the farmers are not just being paid and subsidised to be cruel to cows, now they are being paid to abuse and murder badgers too!

Being a hunt saboteur is dangerous work and activists often receive serious injuries as the clash between crime and compassion meet. Those who care and try to fight for justice and protect the animals suffer at the hands of those who make and break the laws. It is a total disgrace and stain on the UK that this is allowed to happen and those who try to stop it are given no protection at all. So if you take part, take care, stay in numbers, record everything and stay safe.

CHAPTER 38

LIVE BY EXAMPLE

"Don't tell people how to live, demonstrate by example."

- Denis Waitley

This is a very passive form of activism, but again, passive doesn't have to mean ineffective or less powerful. When people see you doing something in a certain way and see how that way is good for you and your health, they will be interested. Peaking someone's interest is a nice way to get them asking questions. When they ask questions because they are interested, you have a head start and are somewhat in a power play. As soon as you get a question, you have an opportunity to answer it in a way that helps the animals. One question usually leads to ten more!

Our epic animal quest is centred around this passive approach. We lead a positive vegan lifestyle and show people that you can travel as a family and live anywhere in the world as a vegan and survive, thrive, and lead an awesome life. We use our day to day activities to show that eating out, shopping, and cooking abroad is easy and in no way an excuse to not go vegan or continue to be vegan when you travel.

This is an important part of what we do and when we started, we came across an article by a successful travel family who isn't vegan and has no intention of being vegan. They wrote a post about how difficult it is to travel as a vegan even though they aren't vegan and never have been! The most ridiculous part was that they said they found it very hard, almost impossible, to eat vegan in London. London!

So it is now our mission to get these people off the top Google spot for the vegan family travel search term. This is so irresponsible to hear someone being so opinionated and final about something that just isn't true. In fact, they told us that we wouldn't be able to eat vegan in Cambodia, and I can tell you that Cambodia is a Vegan paradise! You can't get Linda McCartney sausages or beyond meat burgers, sure, but you get the most delicious vegetables, fruit, soy protein creations and tofu. Everywhere restaurant can create a vegan dish even if not on their menu and the people are so happy to accommodate and help.

We were lucky to attend a Khmer wedding in the rural provinces and in Cambodia, Khmer weddings are big meaty affairs. They eat mostly meat-heavy dishes, and we saw them kill dozens of chickens, a couple of pigs, and even the family cow. This was awful to see, and the night before we were in the pen with the cow hugging her and had no idea they

would eat her. The next day we got up and saw her dis-
membered head on the floor. It was heartbreaking. But even
with so many animals being killed and so much flesh being
cooked and served, the busy cooks didn't forget us vegans
and made us with all the vegetable produce they had. We
were there for two full days and a night and were thoroughly
fed and looked after even. It was a strange experience, and
no different from any wedding anywhere in the world, except
we met the animals they ate. Any wedding we attend anywhere will serve dead animals in the same way, and we doubt
many would offer such an array of Vegan food as we had in
Cambodia, and they certainly wouldn't make as much effort
to make sure we were looked after so well.

So how we act, and especially how we document it, can have
an enormous effect on people looking at us and our work.
This family travel blogger has completely got it wrong but
would say it was her opinion and experience, which of
course, it is. But, the problem is, she is an authority on family
travel, so once she says something is difficult, it almost gives
people permission not to try or find out for themselves and a
pass to give up. When the global situation is so serious and so
many people won't face it, we just don't need this kind of
misinformation on top of everything else the media throws at
us.

One principle that we are passionate about is documenting
not inventing. Documenting is an honest and easy way of
creating content for social media especially video. Rather
than staging things and setting things up or concocting ideas
to create content that is not a true reflection of you and what
you are doing, documenting is what it is. It is a copy of your
actions rather than a designed piece of content that is based
on your intentions of who you want to be or how you would

like to act. Documenting is also good if you don't know where to start making videos, you just record what you are up to and film everything you do. I really like the Vlog style as you can film random thighs throughout the day and intersperse the content with a little speech about what's happening, what you've done, or what you are going to do,

When you invent or 'act as if' you will not come across as genuine and you will just not seem as credible. It may work in the short term, but in the long game, you have to be yourself. Once you start playing to the crowd and making things up or exaggerating, I just think it takes away from your message and doesn't leave a good impression on the viewers. I think about who I like to watch on YouTube or Facebook, and what keeps me coming back again. I see people come and go, but some stay around for many years, and I do think about them differently. I kind of think of the people I've been following for years as friends or colleagues which is weird because I've never spoken to them or interacted with them. But seeing their content for so long has formed a kind of relationship like any other. Once someone in that relationship starts acting or being slightly dishonest or exaggerating, it does put me off them.

We chose a vegan family travel theme for our life and that's something that was important to us, we asked ourselves what we would do if we only had a year left to live and the answer was to travel and see the world and show our children a different life and give them a taste of freedom. Travel isn't everyone's cup of tea, and you can lead by example in your home and life exactly as you are right now. This is again why the Vlog style is so appropriate. It is you living your normal life and sharing it with the world wherever you are. When you get people interested in you and your life, and they see how easy being Vegan is, they have your running narrative reminding them why it is so important to the animals, the planet, and our health, and they will act on it.

When you start living by example and documenting your life, other forms of activism will be included such as animal vigils, animal rescues, and any other activity you carry out because you are a kind and compassionate person. Seeing someone doing something is a great way to be inspired, and so if you show people that you are helping the animals, they might be inclined to do it too.

CHAPTER 39

EVERYDAY ACTIVISM

"With the new day comes new strength and new thoughts."

- Eleanor Roosevelt

I noticed that the idea of using these simple and passive methods of everyday activism have been accused of being 'lazy' or being the work of 'slactivists'. But the idea is not to only implement these every day activism ideas into your activism, but rather to do it in addition to everything else we discuss in this book! Because of this, they deserve a place in the book and as simple as they are, they shouldn't be ignored, discounted or left out of our Vegan activist lifestyle. Here they are . . .

Stickers on laptops

When you are out and about, in coffee shops, university, school or the workplace, placing stickers on the top of your laptop can be a great way to get a website address or simple message across to people who you don't even have to engage and interact with. Passive doesn't translate to ineffective, and if a sticker on a laptop can peak someone's interest enough for them to visit a website or Facebook page that advocates for animal rights and they use the new information they discover to make lifestyle decisions that favour the animals, well then we have success on our hands!

Perhaps they saw the website address elsewhere but didn't look it up, but then when seeing it again on your laptop and maybe again somewhere else, then this could be what they needed. Exposing people repeatedly to messages that cause them to act is marketing 101. If we think of ourselves as marketing machines, then we can be patient and realise that these small actions, carried out repeatedly over time, by many people, really do make a difference and this is how change is made. Of course, we won't change the world by only stickering up our laptops, but when it's in addition to everything else we are doing, it is absolutely effective and worth doing.

Carry information cards

Bring along business cards everywhere you go so that if you get into conversations or debates with interested people, you can pass them some details so they can follow up what you discussed and explore the animals rights issues further. You can make your own business cards and include links to your own content and links to documentaries or organisations that you feel will help people to make the connection.

If you don't want to print your own, then you can order some flyers from organisations like Viva.org and other animal rights groups. These can be totally free, or sometimes you just need to pay the postage. Other sites like the Vegan Society have templates all ready to send to the printers in PDF form.

You could also make up a small card digitally and keep it on your smartphone, then when you exchange Facebook or email details with a new person interested in Veganism, you can send them a copy digitally. We have blog posts and usually send the link to one that matches the conversation we had or a generic link to our Vegan resources page (it's like a starter pack for interested Vegans) that is full of documentaries, books, articles, and YouTube video links. Please feel free to use this or create your own.

Buttons

Much like t-shirts, wearing buttons and badges on your clothes or bags is a great way to attract attention and add the global pool of animal rights messages. People don't have to look at them, but if they do, they might be interested enough to find out what it means and why you are wearing it. Using apparel as conversation starters is a nice easy and chilled way to break barriers and invite conversation. You won't be going into someone else's space and starting a conversation they never planned nor wanted to have. Instead, they are initiating it, and that can often result in a much better debate or discussion.

Car stickers

Your car is a moving billboard, and if you can display a Vegan animal rights message on it, then you will reach potentially thousands of people as you drive around during a typical day. If you are a taxi or Uber driver or work in the transport industry, imagine how many people will see a simple car window sticker, bumper sticker, or window drawing that you place on your vehicle? If you take passengers, why not place some cards or flyers in the back or go even further and put a small TV screen in the back and take advantage of having a captive audience!

Wear T-Shirts

Wearing a Vegan t-shirt is a great way to peak peoples interest and prompt questions without you having to start the conversation. If people are interested or curious, they can ask about the slogan or message you display, and if they are not, they can just ignore you. This is something we don't do as much as we should but mostly because we have a limited and minimalist wardrobe as we are a full-time travel family. But as I replace my old t-shirts, they will have Vegan animal rights themes on them for sure.

When you were a t-shirt, hat, or any item of clothing with a message, you are displaying what you believe in, what you are passionate about, and your commitment to making a difference for the animals. Be proud and use this simple method of everyday activism to make a statement and get more attention to the movement.

Jewellery

Jewellery makes great gifts so you could support local animal rights artists who make jewellery or order online for your friends and family. Wearing jewellery with a message is just like all the other everyday activism ideas, and if it's shiny, someone will notice it and ask about it!

Tattoo

There are not many things more permanent than a tattoo! This takes sticking and jewellery to a whole new level, and if you want to make a lasting statement then this is for you! Obviously, it bloody hurts, and if you are like me and hate the pain that tattoos bring, you could just opt for a small one.

Tattoos are very personal and meaningful, but curious people will very often ask about the meaning of tattoos they see so we have yet another opportunity to talk about Veganism. My activist friend and I went to get Vegan tattoos when we were in Cambodia, and for me, it signified the work we did together and our commitment to the animals and animal activism. She was braver than me and got a pretty big one on her back whereas I got a very small one on my arm. I think it will be cool to get more tattoos from different countries as we travel around and meet new people.

Getting a tattoo is fun, meaningful, and everlasting and if this is something you are into, then it's such a powerful way to show the world you mean business and that animal activism isn't a hobby or a game. Show the world it's a fight for justice for animals everywhere and one that you are not afraid to be a part of.

Get Active In Animal Activism

As we mentioned at the beginning, these everyday activism ideas are not things we should do on their own if we want to make a big impact, but rather, to do in addition to the activism we are already involved with. There are no prizes for the best activists and no rules or bureaucracy - that's what makes it so powerful - but the more active we can be and the more of us who get involved, the better. On top of this, the more skills and ideas we can bring to animal activism, the greater the attention we will be able to attract, and the more people will see our message and hopefully make the connection for the animals.

CHAPTER 40

START A BEEHIVE

"No matter how small you start, start something that matters."

- Brendon Burchard

It's easy for us to criticise other charities as we have done previously in this book, and it's easy to talk about things that don't work without making a better suggestion and giving it a try ourselves. That's why we are building a Beehive right now and trying a different approach to the Dog Meat Trade in Cambodia. It may not work, we might not be successful, but we are going to give it a try and work with the best teams in the country to try. Many projects operate in similar ways to our Beehive concept, so it is not an entirely new way to approach a problem, but I think it isn't done in the charitable world enough and in the nuanced ways we have put across in this book. With this in mind, I thought I should include our

Beehive approach in this book on activism and provide a few chapters of it at the end of the book for you to read for free. .

It would be amazing if others tried the Beehive approach and looked for problems they think it could be applied to. Maybe you could even start one in your community!? Is there something you see that you think you could do better or is there a problem that needs solving that you think you could build a Beehive around? At first, it doesn't cost anything except your time and passion to find out and try. If you don't want to start your own, then join ours! The dog meat project will be ongoing, and as we travel around the world working with other animal problems, there will always be something to join in with. The chances are that there other groups and collaborations happening around you but they just don't put a name to what they are doing. I would argue that they are not as easy to find as a charity, but could well be out there.

We really appreciate you reading this book and hope you will join our Book Club where we are growing our community to make a difference for the animals. We want to take what we experienced and learned in Cambodia and scale it up and are going to give it everything we have to make it work. If we can push the idea of community action and collaboration, and support people and groups in their communities as we travel around, I think we can make a difference in a unique way. We have always dreamed of having a community like this and we are going to give it everything we have to build it into something unique that can really change the world for the animals we meet. We can do something truly unique here, and we have an opportunity to do it together. If we each bare witness to the problems facing animals around the world and pledge a monthly contribution to help them, take action together, and do something about what we see, then we really can change things for them. We always say that alone we can make a difference, but together, we can change the world!

The Beehive is about working together for a common goal and doing it because we are passionate about solving common problems and helping people and other animals in need. I couldn't think of any better way to end this book other than by saying thank you, and that people like us, help animals like these, and we do it together! We want to change the world, and we want to do it with you!

CHAPTER 41

CHANGE THE WORLD

"No matter what people tell you, words and ideas can change the world."

- Robin Williams

I write about changing the world and making it a better place so much that I thought I should go into more detail about just how we can do it! Often, saying something is as far as we go, so I really wanted to actually detail how my family and I are taking action and how you can too!

Change doesn't have to happen immediately and on a massive scale. Change can be as simple as changing your own behaviour in one very specific area. Change can be changing your mindset, and then every action that follows will be influenced by it. Our actions are most often caused by our conscious thoughts and decisions, so if we can change our thoughts, it follows that we can change our actions too.

To change the World for the better, though, that must require much more than a simple change in mindset, right? Not necessarily. I came to the realisation that to be truly compassionate, we had to show compassion for all beings, at all times, in all places. Note beings, this is the key for me. Not just humans, but all beings, all animals and sentient creatures that live and share this World with us. This simple realisation has changed my world, my families world, and a number of other sentient beings world too. Since going vegan, my family have spared the lives of 2,900 animals.

To change the World, we simply might have to make someone's life better. Again, that someone is not limited to human. The someone could be a mouse, a cat, an elephant, or a bird. If you find a bird with a broken wing, you have two choices. Number one, walk by and hope that someone else will take on the problem and care for the bird or number two, pick up that bird, wrap him or her in your scarf or jacket, and take them to a Vet or Wildlife sanctuary for treatment. Once treated, you can take them home and care for them until they are well enough to be released back where you found them. If this is not safe to so, you should take the advice of the professionals and even consider offering a forever home. All too often, we rely on other people to take the action we wish we would take ourselves. I say we have to stop this and that we have to take on the action ourselves. We have to be responsible for helping when we are perfectly capable of helping. Imagine how the bird would feel if you took the time, inconvenienced yourself for a while, and spent just a little money to enable them to fly again? The World, from the birds perspective, is now completely different and you changed it for the better. You did that.

Now, what if someone saw you? What if they had walked by the bird and ignored his or her soft cries for help? Your actions may inspire that person to help the next bird they see in a park on the walk home after work. The next time they see a small injured bird, they might gently scoop them up and follow your lead. Someone sees them, and they too act. Those birds meet each other, sing, mate, and breed more birds and soon the park is filled by the beautiful chorus of compassion.

Something similar to this actually happened to us in Cambodia. We were visiting the local Pagodas to give care, food, and check-ups on cats and dogs that were abandoned and lived there. On one particular visit, we came across a cat that had a very badly broken leg. We had been numerous times before and had never seen him. The Pagodas can be quite large, and each time we visit we come across new animals that have been born there, found refuge themselves, or were abandoned by local people. We took the cat - who we later called Thomas - to three vets to get checked out, x-ray and eventually operated on.

Unfortunately, he had to have his leg amputated as the break was so bad and he had had it for a long time. He is now adopted into a forever home full of love and safety and will soon go to live in Canada. If we didn't change our lives, move to Cambodia, commit to helping animals, and then regularly visit the Pagodas, what would have happened to Thomas? The chances are his leg would have got infected, no one would have treated the infection, and he would have died a sad, painful, and lonely death. Giving up some time, compassion, a little money, and most importantly, taking action, was all we needed to do to help Thomas and we feel incredibly proud of being a part of his story.

We later went on to work with a local Social Enterprise, called Animal Mama, and other individuals who formed a community action group to help the animals at numerous pagoda. Many cats get adopted from the Pagodas now, and the adoption rates are on the increase. Now, this initiative is spreading across the other Pagodas in Phnom Penh, Cambodia and the community action is making a very real and growing difference in the world. This didn't happen overnight, and instead took months with much input, energy, and action from many people that are still needed to grow it further.

Changing the World is not something you have to do in one action or a short space of time. History is composed of, As Leo Tolstoy wrote, 'an infinitely large number of infinitesimally small actions.' An ocean is not made up of one single unit of water, rather a countless series of minute droplets. If we want to see a world flooded with compassion, we only have to add our own droplets to the pool. Drip, drip, drip day after day, year after year, encouraging others to add to our communal reservoir until the waters swell and the dams break. Over time, our individual droplets might grow as we move forward and expand our actions. Our droplets could become thimbles, our thimbles cups until soon we find ourselves emptying compassion by the bucket load.

It is very cliche to bring in Gandhi, but how can I write a post about changing the World and leave his famous quote out of it? If we want to change the world then we first have to change ourselves. Change begins in our mind, then through our actions, it is realised. We can encourage others to change and join us on our quest, and we can help them change knowingly or unknowingly. What do I mean by this? Take Veganism. If we want to encourage other people to Go Vegan there are many routes we can take; some perhaps more successful than others. One thing I could do would be to invite my friends for a delicious meal and not even bring up the idea that it will be completely plant-based. I could cook a lavish Indian meal with many options and choices and really give them a meal to remember. That evening, ten people have not bought, hunted, consumed, or killed, any animal. If ten people ate a chicken dinner, then at least two chickens would have had to be killed, and many cows and chickens would have suffered for the dairy and eggs. That evening, no deaths, no exploitation, and no cruelty. As a bonus, my friends would be surprised at how nice the food tasted, how good they felt afterwards, and how much choice they had. They might ask questions about being Vegan, and I get the opportunity to talk rationally with a receptive, open-minded, and thoughtful group of friends who have unwittingly been shown how awesome Veganism really is.

Our approach is just this, but maybe our story is a little more unorthodox. We live a positive Vegan lifestyle, and our blog is full of posts about Veganism, activism, ethics and morality, plant-based food, travel, lifestyle, world schooling, and much more. You don't have to sell everything you own and move to Cambodia to start a World Wide minimum 10-year trip to make a difference. You can change the world from your own home and start in your own community. The internet has offered us a window to the whole world, and if we get our message right, it can be received by millions of people.

So what can you do right now to make a change in your world? Who can you help and who's life can you make better? All you have to do is commit to Veganism and animal activism, encourage others to withdraw their consent so that they no longer pay for death and suffering, and then show them the alternatives. Take the small steps that need to be made and keep on walking. Gather encouragement and support from fellow like-minded activists along the way and don't be afraid to ask for help, and certainly don't be afraid to give it. These simple steps are all you need to do. One person really can make a difference, but together, we can change the world!

THE END

*. *. *   *   *

Find our more about our Book Club and help the animals today!

www.epicanimalquest.com/club

ACKOWLEDGEMENTS

To all the people involved in animal activism all around the world for everything you are doing to help the animals who need us so badly.

To the Cornwall Animal Rights group who inspired us to get active and get involved and showed us what it means to be compassionate.

To our Book Club members who are part of a community that we are growing together to make a difference for the animals.

To Dr Lucy Haurissa, who this book is dedicated to, for everything she is doing for the animals and human animals in Cambodia, and for being my friend and fellow activist.

To all the team at Animal Mama and our friends Yulia & Darren for inspiring us to do more and teaching us about friendship and standing up for what we believe in while staying true to ourselves.

ABOUT EPIC ANIMAL QUEST

OUR MISSION

Our mission is to lead by example to influence others to show compassion, respect and care for all animals.

Our Main Goals

- We want to leave the world better than we found it.
- We want to stop contributing to the destruction of the planet.
- We want to teach compassion, kindness and care for all living creatures.
- We want to promote a Healthy lifestyle.
- We want to do everything we can to give our children and future generations a brighter future.

Why Are These Goals Important To Us?

We have children and like all parents we want to give them the best we can. We believe this is not achieved through gifts or money, but rather through real world education, teaching them all about a healthy lifestyle, leading by example, sharing experiences, and spending as much time together as possible.

If we can teach the next generation about compassion and how to show it to all animals, we believe this will have a direct effect on how they treat other people. It will positively effect the environment and their own health and well being. By showing compassion for animals we will automatically instil compassion for our fellow humans and bring everyone together regardless of race, colour, nationality or ethnicity.

Compassion for all animals brings with it benefits to diet and health, the environment, and our relationships with other people.

Animals and The Environment

We have lost our connection with most animals and have commodified many of them. Animals are treated as mere objects and are considered as a just a product to be traded and profited from. This has to stop and we have to reconnect with all animals and stop all cruelty wherever we find it.

Starting with our own children and the next generation, we believe we can set them up to start putting right the terrible things we have done to other animals and our planet. There is too much at stake to just carry on regardless. The oceans could be empty of fish by 2050, the rainforests are being destroyed at a sickening pace (2 football fields every second), and over 3000 animals are killed every second just for us to eat them.

The World Is Full Of Good People

We want to highlight the great work that good people are doing everyday and the sacrifices they make with no benefit to themselves. The world can be a cruel and heartless place, but there are millions of good, kind, generous people out there that we want to meet and share their stories with you and the world.

Remove The Wool From Our Eyes

We live in a polarised world. We see cruelty and hate at one end and compassion and love at the other. In between lies the middle ground where most of us carry on with our normal lives without really thinking about the bigger picture. There is nothing wrong with this, it is, after all, how we have been brought up and we are continually bombarded with propaganda from the government and the organisations that own and control our media, our food, and our pharmaceuticals. We believe what we have been told by our parents and authorities and do what we believe is right for us and our family based on what we've been told.

We all have the ability to reason, debate, question, investigate, and explore yet we can so easily be manipulated to follow the crowd, do as we are told, and be convinced by others who try to make us follow their agenda.

We have realised that the world is nothing like the one we were told about. Our human race acts as if it is far more advanced than any other species. We are technologically incomparable but how do we behave ethically? We treat other species as if they are nothing, worthless, and ours to neglect, eat, abuse, and show a complete disregard for. We may be technologically superior but we are lacking ethically, morally, and compassionately.

The internet has developed so much now, so much that we can now remove the wool that has been so cleverly pulled over our eyes. We can see clearly for the first time. We can see how we've have been misled, mis guided, and out right lied to for so long but now it's time we take back our planet, save our fellow animals, and move forward as a cohesive planet of ethical and compassionate human beings.

Life Is For Living

Life doesn't have to be a set pattern of school, college, university, job, retirement, die. You don't have to work for 40-50 years looking forward to retirement only to find that you either don't live long enough to retire or you are too ill to enjoy when you get there! The world has changed, for the worst but also for the better. The internet has provided opportunities to bring people together across the continents and we can use this amazing tool to achieve our goals and live a purposeful and exciting life, helping others less fortunate than ourselves (that's all animals including us humans) and promoting compassion. This might well be the only life we get so we don't want to waste it following the norms society guides us towards. We want to leave our mark on the world and make that mark a positive one.

We believe in this so much that we sold our business, sold almost everything we owned, and committed to a life of travel and adventure in our Quest to help as many animals as we can. If we want to stop the destruction of the environment and stop the cruelty to animals, we have to dedicate our lives to this project.

If You Share Our Philosophy Then Join Our Epic Animal Quest.

We want others to follow our quest and join us on our mission to show compassion, respect and care for all animals.

Help us to help the helpless and shine a light on the good people that represent what it really means to be human.

Join our club: www.epicanimalquest.com/club

Find us at: www.epicanimalquest.com

Email us: lee@epicanimalquest.com or epicanimalquest@gmail.com

Twitter: http://www.twitter.com/epicanimalquest

Instagram: http://www.instagram.com/epicanimalquest

Pinterest: https://uk.pinterest.com/epicanimalquest/

Facebook: https://www.facebook.com/epicanimalquest/

JOIN OUR BOOK CLUB

Do you believe that when you donate money to an animal charity or cause, your money should go directly to the animals?

We do too!

That's why we started our Epic Animal Quest Book Club and why we adopted a community action approach to helping the animals around the world.

How Does The Book Club Work?

SUBSCRIBE	RECIEVE GOODIES	HELP ANIMALS	TRANSPARENCY	MAKE A CHANGE
Join our community action on a level you are comfortable with	You get books & goodies to download every month	We give up to 88% of your subscription to specific animals in need*	You see all the receipts, monthly accounts, and the actual animals being helped!	Together, we make a real difference for the animals and change their world!

What Do You Get?

1   You see exactly how your subscription helps specific
     animals and causes around the world
2   Up to 94% of your subscription goes to the rescued
     animals who need it the most
3   A monthly downloadable animal, travel, recipe or
     food-themed book
4   Giveaways and discounts from our friends and spon-
     sors
5   Exclusive access to competitions and bonuses
6   Access to a private Facebook group
7   Be the first to read the books
8   Help the animals!

How Will We Use The Money?

As we write this book and publish in 2018, we are currently
active in 3 Main Projects.

1. In September 2018, we travel back to Cambodia to rescue
10+ dogs from a dog meat slaughter house and find them
loving forever homes.

2. We are supporting Hercules (who was tortured, burned,
and left for dead) and other terrible cases of sick, injured,
and abandoned street and pagoda animals with Animal
Mama in Phnom Penh.

3. We are helping Cat Beach in Penang who care for 300
sick, injured, and abandoned cats and kittens. They need
help in all areas of their sanctuary including feeding, medical, and day to day care.

How It Began

During our first 18 months volunteering with animal welfare organisations in Asia, we saw how money can be donated and wasted on unnecessary expenses, mismanagement, and bureaucracy. One charity even told us that they didn't want help solving a particular problem because if they solved it (and they could have), they would not have been able to get more donations or apply for funding. This exposed us to how gross the industry can be. We also saw how small, highly effective and passionate groups were overlooked by international funders in favour of those who fell in line with their own corporate style, methods, and ethos. Lengthy meetings, Expos, events, facade, and fundraising took precedence over the actual frontline work.

Of course, not all charities are like this and we have worked with some great ones, but it painted a dark picture of an industry that we naively expected a lot more of. It made us ask 'how do we know who to trust?' and 'how do we really know how our donations are spent?'

The good news is that there is a bright side to this. We worked with social enterprises, rescuers, and local people to form community action groups and saw a different way that we could go about animal welfare. We saw how powerful communities can be when people come together with their individual resources, money, and skills to solve problems they share and are passionate about solving together. We saw that there really is a better way to make a difference and change the world for the animals together, and discovered something amazing that we neither expected or imagined.

What Do We Do Differently?

We use the Book Club subscriptions to build a community action on a global level and give money directly to animals who need it. We are growing a community that is passionate about solving problems that animals face all around the world. As we travel and work with local organisations, shelters, groups, and individual rescuers, we seek out the ones who are effective and need help the most, get involved, and help them as much as we can. We only spend the money on things the animals need and we never just give the money away.

How Much Goes Directly To The Animals?

Gratitude and transparency are important to us so we document everything and share with you the accounts, receipts, photos and video of the work being carried out so you can see for yourself EXACTLY how our community action makes a difference. Our sustainable and scalable social enterprise model means that we can give up to 88% of the subscription money to animals who need it and we fund ourselves through the sale of the books and sponsorships (a further ongoing 25% of sales profits are used for the animal projects). This is a highly efficient use of the money with no expenses, no bureaucracy, and no misuse of your hard earned money.

Join The Club!

We can do something truly unique here and we have an opportunity to do it together. If we each bare witness to the problems facing animals around the world and pledge a monthly contribution to help them, take action together, and do something about what we see, then we really can change the world for the better. People like us come together to do things like this, so join our Club and get involved for the animals today!

How To Join

Choose your monthly membership and join our community action on a level you are comfortable with and then we will send you books, goodies, links, and updates.

Thank You!

Thank you for joining our community action and making a difference. We can't wait to send you awesome books and share the amazing stories of all the animals who we will help together.

From Lee, Rachael. & Family

JOIN HERE: www.epicanimalquest.com/club

BEEHIVE
FREE CHAPTERS

You can buy the full book here: http://epic-animalquest.com/vegan-books/

INTRODUCTION

The Beehive is all about serving ideas to solve problems. It's based on community action and the idea that if we collaborate we can achieve so much more than we ever could on our own. We present it as an alternative to the traditional charity model and encourage anyone thinking of starting a charity to look at the different options available to them. Community action is a powerful approach that we can use to solve social problems, and it allows social enterprise, individuals, businesses, charities, and other groups to work together. When we approach social problems with the Beehive, we can remove many of the issues charities face in their operations and execution, and provide a compelling alternative to what can be an inefficient and outdated model.

The Beehive is formed around some core criticisms of the traditional charity model and argues that if we could remove the negative aspects of charitable organisations, and encourage more collaboration between them and other groups, businesses, and social enterprises, then we could find a better way to solve social problems and do it in a way where everyone involved wins; especially those experiencing the problems!

Before we start, I have to stress that my criticism is not of every individual charity. But it is a criticism of the ineffective, inefficient, wasteful, non-transparent, unethical, and ungrateful ones. There are amazing charities doing fantastic work all around the world, and they are achieving things for animals I could never imagine doing. We have worked with some and will continue to, but the charity model, on the whole, is outdated, it has many flaws, and we believe there is a better way. The people involved in ineffective charities are not purposefully running them to be like this. However, when they copy a charity model that doesn't work, and have no experience in business or management, and then start to lose the passion they began with due to the stresses charity work can involve, they will have a high chance of failure; much like any regular business would. The difference is, we don't feel so sorry for businesses and can freely criticise them for their failings. But when a charity fails, we seem to be more reserved in our criticism, and the donors most often get the blame, not the people who founded the charity or the model it was based on. This has to stop, and if we see something that doesn't make sense, we should speak out about it, especially if we deem it to be unethical.

We want to share the Beehive concept with you, but to do it, we have to strip down the idea of charity and highlight some serious issues we have personally experienced and seen reported by others in the industry. Then we can show why we feel the Beehive is an alternative model that we should consider if we want to make real lasting and sustainable changes in the world. The problems we have experienced are not unique to us, and we have discussed them with many other people who have been involved in the charity sector.

My preference in life is to be positive, help build others up and not bring them down, but we should never ignore the negatives we encounter. Instead, I believe we should confront them, put them out into the open, analyse them, reflect on them, discuss them, and then learn from them so that we don't make the same mistakes ourselves. The world is made up of good and bad experiences, good and bad people, and good and bad situations. Good people can end up doing bad things, and what can start off as a good cause can end up being a damaging one. We are continually being tested and have to decide where to align ourselves. I find myself in a position where we have to share some negative experiences in order to develop and champion a positive way forward and one that could bring more people together than ever before. Of course, some people might take offence to this book, but it is not my intention to give it, and I can't be responsible for those who choose to take it. This book is merely an observation based on our experiences and a suggestion to try something new.

I've heard it said that the world doesn't need more critics, but rather it needs more creators. While I agree with this, I also feel that to introduce new creations and ideas, we have to critique the old ones; especially if we think they aren't working as well as they could - and should - be. If we see things that don't work as well as we think they could, and we see donors being misled and their donations being wasted, isn't our obligation to point this out, put forward a better idea, and then work hard to implement it? I believe it is, so here is our Beehive concept where we serve the idea to solve the problem.

Thank you so much for everything you are doing to help the animals and thank you for choosing my book to be part of your journey. Please enjoy reading and I would love it if you joined me on:

Facebook: www.facebook.com/epicanimalquest/
Email: lee@epicanimalquest.com
Website: www.epicanimalquest.com

Thank you

Lee

SECTION 1

COMMUNITY ACTION

CHAPTER 1

GOOD FOR THE BEEHIVE

"Alone we can do so little; together we can do so much."

- Helen Keller

Serve the idea, solve the problem. What does this mean exactly? Beehive is based on the concept of community action, working together without a leader to solve a problem that we are all passionate and capable of solving. On our own, we couldn't solve the problem, but together, by sharing our time, skills, and resources, we can. The Beehive represents this community. It's made up of all the individual people, groups, and organisations who want to solve a particular problem and these people with their skills, time, and efforts, are the bees. This book makes the case that what is good for the beehive is also good for the bee. When we come together to solve common problems and work together in our own ways to do it, we can achieve much more than we ever could on our own.

This is certainly not a new concept, and the idea of the whole being greater than the sum of its parts has been around a long time. But I just don't think people relate to that idea as much as they ought to. I also want to come away from the idea of conformity and organisational structures and move more towards creators, problem solvers, and people who get things done. We are seeing more and more in the various industries how freelance workers and specialists are hired as individuals to work on individual projects. Take the movie industry. An independent writer will create the story, a producer will purchase it, then a screenwriter will adapt it,   and then numerous outside agencies will be brought together to film it, work on the special effects, and carry out the stunts. Instead of a single film company doing all of these tasks, individuals and specialist companies are each hired for what they can do and their specific skills. They provide their own small component of the overall movie, and once the film is complete, they split up and move on. They may work with each other again in the future, but maybe not. Although this is an excellent example of individuals and individual skills coming together to solve a problem - or make something in this case - it still revolves around a direct-or and set of producers. Our Beehive is different because it has none of these roles and none of the problems they bring.

The Beehive aims to show that the whole doesn't need a defined leader, director, or even a producer. Sure, we may need an instigator, a coordinator, and a central hub from which to operate, but community action is about serving the idea and not some self-ordained leader or carefully chosen hierarchy. We want to share and give away credit to everyone involved rather than take all the credit as the lead of a pro-ject or exercise that didn't need us.

How many small businesses and charities do you know that have a 'founder'? Some people may be in a business where they have two to five members of staff, or even just work on their own. They call themselves the Founder or the Director, and their team refers to them in this way too. The team starts to look up and be in awe of their new 'Queen

Bee' (or King Bee, but that doesn't really fit the analogy!) They have meetings to decide how they will be introduced at other meetings and what names and titles should appear on their fancy new business cards, and as they do this, their focus dwindles ever so slowly away from the problem they set out to solve. What started as the primary focus - the most important element in the equation - now becomes second to the oh so important name and title on the business card.

The Beehive concept places the idea (or solution) we all share to solve a problem we all want to solve as the most important element above everything else. This is our 'Queen Bee'. We serve the idea, the project, the solution, and never a person or Founder. Another key part of the Beehive is that we don't volunteer to be part of a community action; instead, we participate in it and on our own terms. We don't have to work a set number of hours, turn up at a set time, or follow any set of policies and procedures. We just do what we can to serve the idea and help to solve the problem in ways that we think will help. Some people will give more, some less, but it doesn't matter; it's not a competition. As long as we are all doing something that feeds the idea, then we are all part of the Beehive. Anyone can leave at any time without having to give notice, write a letter, or hurt anyone's feelings. It's a freedom to act alongside other passionate people who want to solve the same problems.

Tolstoy said that change is 'an infinitesimal number of acts carried out over an infinite time.' The acts of many individuals over time create change and not the acts of one King or Queen. This makes change fluid, viscous, and ever evolving. Things don't go from state A to state B because of the will or decry of one person. Of course, the idea of one person can spark a revolution, but that revolution comes from the acts of many. When these acts start to all come together and have an effect that steers the change towards a common goal, then we see group action - community action - at work. What we start off with and where we think we may end up, can be completely different from where we may find ourselves in the future. And this isn't a bad thing! The will and input of many can make the results that we all wanted; whether we know it or not.

The Beehive can self-correct as the bees get buzzy (sorry, I promise there won't be bee puns throughout) and go about their individual tasks. If the hive is taking a shape that is not appealing, the actions can be changed with little friction. No need to change policies or working practices, just a discussion and agreement on how to carry on and then we get on with it. If one thing doesn't work, it doesn't matter, and we haven't risked everything by trying it. As the Beehive is built, groups, organisations, and individuals within the hive can serve the idea in their own ways, and if some of those ways don't work, then there will be many more surrounding them that can hold up the structure and carry on building around them. As one individual idea works, it can be replicated and copied by other bees if they choose to. We go into this abstract idea of Hexagonal thinking and the Beehive structure in a later chapter.

The Beehive is built on some core principles, with community action being the most important. For it to work, we have to develop our community actions on the ideals of collaboration, sharing, gratitude, abundance mindset, compassion, and with a tribe mentality. The Beehive favours social enterprise, hands-on actions, and a grassroots approach. Everyone in the Beehive is treated equally, with no hierarchy, and everyone is accountable, responsible, and a part of the success or failure and the rewards that come with each. The Beehive strives for efficiency, effectiveness, as well as monitoring and evaluation of the work, and all of this is delivered in a way that is transparent and open as possible. No one takes ownership or possession so that the work may be copied and replicated with no restrictions.

When you have been part of a community action, no matter how small or how many people took part, you get a sense of achievement like you have never had before. It feels incredible to see other people working on a problem without getting paid, without direct gain, and without seeking personal glory. When passionate people come together with no other motive other than solving a common problem, it will blow you away! Community action showed me that there is a different way to achieve results and get things done. It taught me the power of passion, compassion, and determination. It introduced me to friends who are now my family, and it led me in a direction that would totally change my life. But it's not for everyone . . . . .

CHAPTER 2

COMMUNITY ACTION

"We make a living by what we get, but we make a life by what we give."

- Winston Churchill

We first came across the concept of 'community action' during our time in Cambodia. Community action is some-thing we had never experienced before, and it was fascinating to see how it worked and just how effective it could be. When we first started Epic Animal Quest, we imagined we would travel around volunteering with charities, shelters, and sanc-tuaries and help them raise money for their causes; and for a time we did just that. But after spending six months volun-teering with a charity in Cambodia and further twelve months getting an insight into how international charities worked with other smaller, local ones, we were disillusioned.

Even though we didn't agree with a lot of what we were seeing, we thought that this had to be the way to do things. Although both Rachael and I worked for social charities in the UK, we had never worked with animal welfare. Some charities we were experiencing were well trusted and respected and came with endorsements from other larger charities, so we believed they were the experts and that we should follow their lead. After all, who were we to come along with no experience in the animal welfare sector and start making a ruckus?

But, after eighteen months, we felt we had learned and seen enough, and we thought there had to be another way to get things done because what we saw just wasn't working. It seemed like a flawed model, with too many negative aspects and not enough positives. With much room for error and bad decision making, yet few barriers for entry, it seemed to us that anyone could start a charity or nonprofit, gather donations, but end up not solving the problems they set out to because they drowned themselves in bureaucracy and got tangled up in their own red tape. Donations seemed to get used less and less for the animals, and more and more on the organisation, unnecessary overheads, and Human Resources.

Luckily, we started to get involved with a social enterprise called Animal Mama, a veterinary clinic and pet wellness centre that uses profits to help sick, injured, and abandoned street and pagoda animals as well as providing affordable pet care for locals who would never otherwise afford it. They blew us away with their level of passion, compassion, activity, and positivity.

The impact they were having on the community and the number of animals they were helping, were both far greater than anything we had seen anywhere else in Phnom Penh - even Cambodia - and they were doing it without any financial support using only their profits, own money, and a few random donations from a small group of dedicated supporters in the community. Any donations they received went straight to an animal - all of it, every penny - and because they were set up as a social enterprise, they didn't need to use the donations to raise more money, pay for expenses, bills, overheads, or any costs other than what was required by the animals in their care. They inspired us to think about animal welfare differently, and the more we worked with them, the more we learned about the concept of community action. Once we saw it in action, we knew this was how we should get involved. We started to meet other people like us, individuals who wanted to do something to help the animals and make a difference, and we began to have hope.

Since then, we have been developing the idea of community action and came up with our Beehive concept to encapsulate everything we learned and experienced. It all starts with community action and so I think it would be useful to define it in a simple sentence before we go any further. When we talk about community action, we define it as:

'Campaigns that are undertaken by the people living in a particular place.'

It shouldn't be confused with the political descriptions used in the UK and US. The community action we are passionate about is the concept of like-minded people coming together sharing their own time, money, resources, and skills to make a difference and solve problems. You could even think of it as a way of crowdfunding compassion! This is the simplest definition that sums it up in one sentence, but there is much more to it. We believe that we don't have to live in a specific place to be part of a community or take responsibility. Communities can exist virtually and can bring people together from all countries and all walks of life. When we identify a common problem, we can look for other like-minded people who are passionate about solving it, and we can work together to do it. This can be in the form of resource and information sharing, giving our time and money, sharing our expertise, spreading the word and encouraging others to join. We don't have to physically live or be located in a particular area to be part of the community, and the community is more a mental construct than a physical one; no boundaries, no borders, but instead a fluid ever growing and evolving state of co-existence and constant action around a common problem.

There is an excellent example of Community Action in the book, and the movie trilogy, The Lord of The Rings. Community Action is just like a fellowship. We may all be from entirely different backgrounds, countries, religions, belief systems, and professions, but we share a common belief that doing the right thing is always the right thing. When we know about something, we have to act and can't turn our backs. When we try to ignore it, it eats away at us, and we have to do something about it; no matter how frustrated it makes us. No one gets paid, and we do it knowing that collaboration is to key to success and that we will all benefit from the outcome. Get that ring to Mordor, and we make the world a better place for everyone - except Saruman of course!

As we form our own fellowships, we will each bring something unique to them. It may be gold coins from like dwarves, specific precision skills like the Elves or the local knowledge, coordination, and connections brought by Gandalf the wizard. Even though we will meet some trolls along the way, we can overcome them together and keep moving forward. We can all come together to make things happen, and although the fellowships can get split up and we may work independently on our own aspects of the journey, we all reach the destination together and because of each other; all serving the common goal to solve a specific problem.

Community action doesn't need a leader, a founder, a board, or even a logo. It can operate through simple communication methods, and everyone can contribute as much or as little as they like. It's not like volunteering, because you aren't volunteering for an organisation, you are working for the animals and for yourself; you participate. When you act for your beliefs and out of compassion and do it with other people who are acting for the same reasons, then you become part of something special that transcends any volunteering experience you could ever have.

Just like the idea of a 'grassroots movement' that we discuss in a later chapter, community action can get hijacked by corporate-style organisations in a bid to come across as being more involved with the community than they really are. This appeals to donors, and a few well thought out photos can create an appealing facade. But it's not true community action, and if the problems are being used to raise more money, then it's purely a marketing and PR exercise. It's easy to see if a community action is not really a community action. Just look at who is involved, who is participating, and what they are doing. Do they come across as doing it together, or is one organisation leading it and taking all the credit? You can also compare the transparency and look and how they use the money they have and raise. Do they share the work of others and is their information specific and verifiable? If they are doing the same job that you know can be done cheaper somewhere else or by another group in the area and field, then why aren't they collaborating with them? True community action stands out, and so does a fake. Look for these things, ask these questions, and you will soon find out for yourself which ones merit your participation.

BEEHIVE
FREE CHAPTERS END

You can buy the full book here: http://epicanim-alquest.com/vegan-books/

Thank you